Generis
PUBLISHING

Statistics, Accounting, and Finance: The Synergy of an Organization Management Success

Dr. Desire Luamba
Dr. Joel Chagadama

Title: Statistics, Accounting, and Finance: The Synergy of an Organization Management Success

ISBN: 979-8-89248-309-4

Author: Dr. Desire Luamba, Dr. Joel Chagadama

Cover image: https://pixabay.com/

Publisher: Generis Publishing
Online orders: www.generis-publishing.com
Contact email: info@generis-publishing.com

Statistics, Accounting, and Finance:

The Synergy of an Organization Management Success

1. **Dr. Desire Luamba**

   DBA-Finance, Vice President and CEO, Start Light Consulting LLC, Manassas, VA-USA

   https://orcid.org/0000-0001-5138-1550

   Email: luambade@gmail.com and Desire@gobrightstar.com

2. **Dr. Joel Chagadama**

   DBA-Finance, President, Start Light Consulting LLC, Manassas, VA-USA

   https://orcid.org/0000-0002-7253-6977

   Email: Jchagadama@hotmail.com

From the Authors

Dear Readers,

Why this book? The authors worked hard to provide this handy material for researchers, students, and business managers. This book contains features to help you learn or understand the basic principles of statistics, accounting, and finance, the three management pillars, and how they can be used to support a business or an organization's success. The tenets, examples, and case studies applied in this book are also helpful whether you are using them in large, middle-sized, small-profit, or nonprofit organizations. The focus is to help our readers reach their personal and organizational goals and build a positive business image for their organizations.

Good luck reading and learning from this book. We hope you enjoy reading it and become involved in it. We can attest that you will not be disappointed. Feel free to contact the authors for any suggestions or questions.

Dr. Desire Luamba

Dr. Joel Chagadama

Author Commitment

Learning. Innovation. Success

Dr. Desire Luamba

Dr. Desire Luamba has worked in the business and financial industries for many years. Dr. Desire Luamba holds a Doctor of Business Administration (DBA) with a concentration in Finance from Walden University, a Master of Business Administration (MBA) with a concentration in Finance from Strayer University, and a Bachelor of Science (BS-Statistics) from the Institut Superieur des Statistiques/ ISS-Lubumbashi/DRC (French-Program). His professional experience includes using financial and statistical tools to make long- and short-term accounting, budgeting, and financial decisions. He advises businesses in analyzing costs, accounting issues, business problems, and financial statements. He also conducts audit work and develops business model plans based on innovation and diversification strategies. He taught finance, statistics, and accounting courses for many years. In addition, he published many articles that can be found on Google Scholar, Academia, and ORCID. He is a fan of teaching, doing research, and playing tennis. He completed much training in business management, statistics, leadership, and audit controls.

Dr. Joel Chagadama

"It's not about having the right opportunities. It's about handling the opportunities right." - Mark Hunter. Dr. Joel Chagadama is an accomplished and seasoned Chief Financial Officer with over a decade of experience. His experience lies in driving teams by developing and implementing strategic financial procedures and systems while establishing effective operational processes to drive business success and control costs. In addition, his expertise includes:

- Spearheaded financial and accounting management, including financial analyses, accounting, due diligence, strategic business planning, forecasting, reporting, budget analysis, and risk management to accelerate overall business success.
- Excelling in various executive-level financial leadership capacities for multiple companies, continually revamping and improving processes, staff, and internal systems to achieve dynamic results.
- Developing and instituting financial policies and procedures that improve cash flow and realize high-impact savings.

His remarkable leadership and interpersonal skills help him communicate with upper management and team members. He is confident in delivering impeccable results through his dedication to handling multiple functions and activities under high-pressure environments and tight deadlines. Dr. Joel Chagadama holds a Doctor of Business Administration (DBA) with a concentration in Finance from Walden University and a Master of Business Administration (MBA-Finance) from Strayer University.

Acknowledgment

We extend our gratitude and appreciation to everyone who has supported us in creating and shaping this book.

This endeavor would not have been possible without the unwavering support and encouragement from all our colleagues, mentors, and friends. Your support and guidance have been instrumental in shaping the content of this book, making it a valuable resource for businesses, students, and researchers alike.

To our esteemed peers and fellow researchers, thank you for your collaboration and valuable insights. Your contributions have enriched the content of this book, reflecting diverse perspectives and cutting-edge knowledge in the fields of statistics, accounting, and finance.

We give special thanks to the businesses and organizations that generously shared their case studies and real-world experiences. Your practical examples have added depth and relevance to the book, providing readers with valuable lessons and inspiration.

To our diligent team of editors, proofreaders, and designers, we are grateful for your meticulous efforts in ensuring the quality and clarity of the book. Your attention to detail and dedication to excellence have played a vital role in making this book accessible and reader-friendly.

We also acknowledge the support of our families and loved ones, who stood by us with unwavering encouragement and understanding throughout the book's creation. Your love and support have been our constant motivation, driving us to bring this project to fruition.

Moreover, we extend our deepest gratitude to our readers, businesses, students, and researchers who will embark on this journey of exploration with us. We hope that the knowledge and insights shared in this book will inspire innovation, creativity, and progress in your respective endeavors.

In conclusion, we acknowledge each person who contributed to the creation of this book, directly or indirectly. Your support and commitment have transformed an idea into a tangible reality, and we are truly grateful for your role in making " **Statistics, Accounting, and Finance: The Synergy for an Efficient Organization Management"** a valuable resource in pursuing knowledge and excellence.

With heartfelt thanks,

Dr. Desire Luamba
Dr. Joel Chagadama

Table of Contents

Acronyms & Abbreviations

ARIMA Autoregressive Integrated Moving Average
CEO Chief Financial Officer
COO Chief Operations Officer
DAR Debt to Asset Ratio
DMV Washington DC, Maryland, and Virginia
EPS Earnings per Share
FER Fundraising Efficiency Ratio
GAAP Generally Accepted Accounting Principles
GDP Gross Domestic Products
IFRS International Financial Reporting Systems
IRR Interest Rate Return
ISC International Salvation Council
KPI Key Performance Indicators
LLC Limited Liability Company
MIS Management Information System
NGO Non-Governmental Organization
NPV Net Present Value
PCA Principal Component Analysis
P&L Profit and Loss
PPE Property, Plant, and Equipment
PSC 7 ELEVEN- Philippines Seven Corporation
ROA Return on Asset
ROE Return on Equity
ROI Return on Investment
SEC Securities and Exchange Commission
SEO Search Engine Optimization
SROI Social Return on Investment
WACC Weighted Average Cost of Capital

ZBB Zero-based Budget

Introduction

Having appropriate and practical managerial tools has become a big concern for organization managers in pursuing success, and this is because of the impacts of globalization and technological advances on business operations. Many studies have shown that globalization and technological advances have increased competitiveness and suggested that a strategic data-driven approach from statistics, accounting, and finance was paramount for organizational sustainability.[1] Then, mastering statistics, accounting, and finance disciplines, three vital management pillars, has become a solution that contributes to achieving organizational goals. The three disciplines form a powerful trio that helps organization managers make informed decisions, optimize operations, and foster growth[2]. Organizations can mitigate challenges, seize opportunities, and ultimately achieve their objectives by exploring the insights from statistics, maintaining sound accounting practices, and leveraging financial acumen.

This book delves into the crucial role of statistics, accounting, and finance in driving organizational success for both profit and nonprofit entities. The authors explored how these disciplines complement each other and create a cohesive framework for effective management. By understanding the significance of data-driven decision-making, the accurate tracking and analysis of financial transactions, and the strategic allocation of resources, organization leaders or managers can optimize their performance and align with their organization's missions and visions.

The authors illustrated the impact of incorporating statistical methods in planning, forecasting, and risk assessment through real-world examples and case studies. We will also examine the pivotal role of accounting in providing a clear financial picture, ensuring compliance with regulatory standards, and fostering transparency and accountability within organizations. Furthermore, the authors explored and presented how financial expertise aids in budgeting, investment decisions, and optimizing capital structures for sustainable growth. At the end of

[1] Harrou, F., Sun, Y., Hering, A. S., & Madakyaru, M. (2020). *Statistical process monitoring using advanced data-driven and deep learning approaches theory and practical applications*. Elsevier.
[2] Raval, V. (2020). *Corporate governance: a pragmatic guide for auditors, directors, investors, and accountants*. CRC Press.

each chapter, we (the authors) presented some exercises for our readers to assess their understanding of the materials included in the chapter.

Join us on this journey to uncover the transformative potential of statistics, accounting, and finance in propelling both profit and nonprofit organizations toward long-term success. By embracing these disciplines and incorporating them into their management practices, organizations can mitigate uncertainty risks, maximize efficiency, and foster a culture of continuous improvement that ultimately benefits all stakeholders involved in the organization's success and viability.

Section 1:

The Role of Organization, Statistics, Accounting, and Finance

Chapter 1

The Role of an Organization

1.1 Introduction

Organizations and corporations are pillars of progress and innovation, impacting the world in bustling business activities. Organizations should be dynamic entities driven by visionary leadership and collective efforts. Organizations or corporations are the backbone of economies that shape initiatives and influence societies[3]. From large to small organizations, each organization represents a unique ecosystem that brings together diverse talents, resources, and ideas to pursue shared goals or missions.

Organizations play a crucial role in shaping economies and society and can be broadly categorized into two main types: profit and nonprofit organizations. Profit or corporate organizations are driven by the pursuit of profit and shareholder value, while nonprofit organizations aim to serve a social or humanitarian purpose. Despite their objectives, profit and nonprofit organizations share a common need to utilize statistics, accounting, and finance in their management system or business operations[4].

In both cases, effective management is paramount for an organization's success and sustainability. Statistics, accounting, and finance form the cornerstone of decision-making, enabling organizations to understand, assess, and enhance their operations.

Throughout this exploration, we will uncover what makes organizations successful, including their adaptability to innovate and resilience to overcome challenges. We will also discover how organizations function as intricate ecosystems where departments collaborate harmoniously, and individuals contribute their unique skills to achieve a collective purpose.

---

[3] Turner, P. (2022). *Complementarity in Organizations: Strategy, Leadership, Management, Talent and Engagement in the Fourth Industrial Revolution*. Springer Nature.
[4] Dicke, L. A., & Ott, J. S. (Eds.). (2023). *Understanding nonprofit organizations: Governance, leadership, and management*. Taylor & Francis.

Moreover, organizations serve as more than just profit-generating entities. Many embrace corporate responsibility, championing environmental sustainability, social welfare, and ethical business practices. They aspire to be agents of positive change, making a difference not only in the marketplace but also in the lives of their employees, customers, and the global community.

Join us as we unravel the tapestry of organizations and corporations, navigating the complexities of their structures, the dynamics of their leadership, and the vision that propels them toward their future. From traditional hierarchies to innovative flat systems, from family-owned businesses to publicly traded giants, each organization contributes its unique footprint to the diverse corporate landscape.

As we journey through the natural organization environment, we will encounter stories of triumph and challenges, tales of perseverance and innovation, and testimonies of the profound impact they create. As organizations born from the aspirations of visionary minds, the authors will focus on how they should continue to shape our world, leaving a legacy of growth, progress, and transformation.

1.2 What Is an Organization?

An organization is a structured entity formed to achieve specific objectives, carry out defined tasks, or provide certain services. It brings together people, resources, and processes to work towards common goals efficiently and effectively. The primary role of an organization is to coordinate and align various activities, resources, and individuals to achieve its mission and vision[5]. This coordination enables specialization, division of labor, and utilization of resources to optimize productivity and outcomes.

1.3 Types of Organizations

Organizations can be broadly categorized into two main types:

1. Profit Organizations

Profit organizations are businesses and enterprises established to generate profits for their owners or shareholders. Profit organizations are typically private

[5] Chagadama, J. (2022). *Small Construction Business Owners' Strategies to Reduce Voluntary Employee Turnover* (Doctoral dissertation, Walden University).

companies, publicly traded corporations, partnerships, and sole proprietorships[6]. Their focus is creating value for their shareholders by offering goods or services in the market at a price higher than their production costs. The surplus revenue generated after covering expenses is distributed among the stakeholders as profits.

2. Nonprofit Organizations

Conversely, nonprofit entities are established to fulfill social, educational, charitable, religious, or humanitarian missions. They do not have profit generation as their primary objective. Instead, they reinvest excess revenue into their programs and services to further their mission. Nonprofits are often tax-exempt organizations that rely on donations, grants, and other funding sources to sustain their operations and activities.

1.4 Sizes of Organizations

Organizations can be broadly categorized based on their size and scale of operations. The size of an organization is typically determined by factors such as the number of employees, revenue generated, market presence, and overall complexity of its operations.[2] The three main categories of organizations based on size are large, middle-sized, and small.

1. **Large Organizations**: Large organizations are characterized by their significant scale of operations, extensive resources, and widespread market presence. These entities typically employ a large number of people and generate substantial revenue. Large organizations often operate in multiple regions or countries and may have diversified business lines. They are typically well-established and have a strong brand presence. Large organizations include multinational corporations like **Apple, Microsoft, Toyota, Walmart, Amazon, etc.** They also have a complex organizational structure with various departments and hierarchical levels, allowing them to handle extensive operations and serve a vast customer base. In the USA, large organizations generate more than $1 billion and employ at least 500 employees.
2. **Middle-sized Organizations**: Middle-sized organizations, also known as medium-sized or mid-sized organizations, fall between large and small organizations in scale. They are more substantial than small businesses but

[6] Luamba, D. (2019). *Strategies small business owners use to remain sustainable* (Doctoral dissertation, Walden University).

not as vast or complex as large corporations. Middle-sized organizations typically have a moderate number of employees and revenue. They may operate in a specific region or a niche market. These organizations often have a more flexible organizational structure than larger entities, allowing for faster decision-making and adaptability. Middle-sized organizations include regional manufacturing companies, local retail chains, and specialized service providers. In the USA, middle-sized organizations generate revenue between $10 million to $1 billion and have more than 50 employees[1]. Examples of middle-sized organizations include legal, insurance, accounting, or finance firms.

3. **Small Organizations**: Small organizations are characterized by their limited scale of operations, relatively small workforce, and more localized presence. These entities typically have lower revenue compared to their larger counterparts. Small organizations are often entrepreneurial ventures or family-owned businesses that cater to specific local markets or niches. Due to their size, they are often more agile and can respond quickly to changes in the market. Small organizations may have a flatter organizational structure with less bureaucracy, facilitating direct communication between management and employees. Examples of small organizations include neighborhood restaurants, independent boutique stores, and local non-governmental organizations (NGOs).

It's essential to note that the classification of organizations into these categories is not rigid, and there may be variations based on the industry and location. Additionally, the definitions of "large," "middle-sized," and "small organizations" may depend on the specific context or country[7]. Nonetheless, understanding these categories helps provide a general framework for analyzing and comparing organizations based on their size and complexity.

1.5 Why Profit and Nonprofit Organizations Need Sound Management

Regardless of whether an organization is profit-oriented or nonprofit, the need for effective management is crucial for several reasons[8]:

1. **Goal Achievement**

[7] Luamba, D. (2019). *Strategies small business owners use to remain sustainable* (Doctoral dissertation, Walden University).

[8] Blye, M. L. (2020). *Reducing the Frequency and Effects of Fraudulent Activities in Community Action Agencies* (Doctoral dissertation, Walden University).

Good management ensures that an organization's mission, objectives, and strategies are clearly defined and communicated across all levels. It aligns the efforts of employees and resources toward achieving these goals efficiently.

2. **Resource Optimization**

   Good management helps properly allocate and utilize financial, human, and physical resources. It aims to maximize productivity and minimize waste, which is vital for both profitability and the successful delivery of services by nonprofits.

3. **Decision-Making**

   Managers are critical in making informed decisions based on data, market trends, and organizational insights. Informed decision-making leads to better outcomes, reduced risks, and increased adaptability to changing environments.

4. **Financial Stability**

   For-profit organizations need effective financial management to ensure sustainable profitability and growth. Nonprofit organizations require solid financial management to maintain stability, demonstrate fiscal responsibility to donors and regulators, and ensure long-term sustainability.

5. **Stakeholder Satisfaction**

   Successful management fosters positive relationships with stakeholders, such as customers, employees, shareholders, donors, and the community. Satisfied stakeholders lead to increased loyalty, support, and goodwill for the organization.

6. **Adaptability and Innovation**

   Organizations must be adaptive and innovative to stay relevant and competitive in today's rapidly changing world. Good management encourages a culture of creativity, continuous improvement, and forward-thinking[9].

---

[9] Luamba, D. S., Blye, M. L., Mwema, I. E. M., Williams, I. A., James, K., & Chagadama, J. (2021). The benefits of innovation for small businesses. *International Journal of Business and Management Research, 9*(4), 425-432.

1.6 Chapter Summary

Profit and non-profit organizations require effective management to thrive in their respective contexts. Proper management ensures that resources are utilized optimally, goals are achieved, and stakeholders' interests are well served. By implementing sound management practices, organizations can navigate challenges, seize opportunities, and position themselves for long-term success and impact.

1.7 Case Studies

1.7.1 Non-Profit Organization: International Salvation Council (ISC)

Introduction: The International Salvation Council (ISC) is a small NGO serving individuals and families in the Washington, D.C., metropolitan area. ISC's commitment to its mission and effective financial practices have allowed the organization to achieve its goals and impact the community[10].

Mission and Goals: ISC's mission is to provide essential services to those in need, regardless of their background, and to promote well-being and self-sufficiency. The organization's goals include providing interpretation, housing support, counseling services, and immigration and employment assistance to refugees and immigrants in the region [1].

Sound Statistics and Data Management: ISC strongly emphasizes data collection, analysis, and reporting. The organization maintains a robust database that tracks client demographics, program utilization, and outcomes. This data-driven approach enables ISC to monitor its impact, identify trends, and make informed decisions.

Financial Sustainability and Stewardship: ISC's exemplary financial management practices contribute significantly to its ability to fulfill its mission and achieve its goals.

1. **Transparent Financial Reporting**: ISC maintains transparent and accurate financial reporting, providing stakeholders with a clear overview of the organization's financial health. Regular financial statements and reports are shared with the board of directors, staff, donors, and the public.
2. **Diverse Revenue Streams**: The organization has established a diversified funding portfolio, including government grants, private donations, corporate partnerships, and fundraising events. This diversity reduces dependency on a single funding source, ensuring financial stability even in uncertain economic conditions.
3. **Strategic Budgeting**: ISC employs a strategic budgeting process that aligns with its mission and goals. Each program's budget is carefully developed, considering revenue and expenses, and reviewed regularly to ensure alignment with the organization's strategic priorities.

[10] International Salvation Council. (2023). *Missions and goals*. Retrieved from https://intersalvation.org/.

4. **Cost Efficiency**: The organization focuses on cost efficiency without compromising the quality of its services. This is achieved through carefully monitoring expenditures, negotiating vendor contracts, and seeking opportunities for shared resources.
5. **Reserve Fund and Financial Planning**: ISC maintains a reserve fund to buffer against unexpected financial challenges. This prudent approach to financial planning demonstrates the organization's commitment to long-term sustainability.
6. **Internal Solid Controls**: ISC has implemented robust internal controls to prevent fraud and ensure the responsible use of funds. These include regular audits, separation of financial duties, and adherence to ethical accounting practices.
7. **Impact Measurement**: ISC quantifies its impact by tracking key performance indicators and outcomes. The organization uses this data to showcase its effectiveness to stakeholders and make informed decisions about resource allocation.

ISC's sound statistics, accounting, and finance practices are pivotal in enabling the organization to meet its mission and goals effectively. Through transparent financial reporting, diversified revenue streams, strategic budgeting, and prudent financial planning, ISC has established itself as a model for financial management within the non-profit sector. These practices ensure the organization's financial sustainability and contribute to its ability to create a positive and lasting impact on the community it serves.

1.7.2 Profit Organization: Star Light Consulting LLC

Introduction: Star Light Consulting LLC, founded in 2020 by two dedicated doctoral students, Dr. Joel Chagadama and Dr. Desire Luamba, is a small, minority-profit consulting business based in Manassas, Virginia. This case study explores the journey of Star Light Consulting LLC, which specializes in offering financial services to individuals and companies in the DMV area (Washington, DC, Maryland, and Virginia). It examines how the firm achieved remarkable success through innovative strategies, effective organizational structure, and sound leadership management.

Background: In 2020, Dr. Joel Chagadama and Dr. Desire Luamba, both doctoral students passionate about finance and a commitment to making a positive impact, founded Star Light Consulting LLC. They aimed to provide high-quality financial services to a diverse clientele while overcoming challenges associated with their small, minority-owned status.

Challenges Faced

1. **Limited Visibility**: Star Light Consulting LLC faced the challenge of establishing visibility and credibility in a competitive consulting industry.
2. **Financial Constraints**: The founders had limited financial resources, initially restricting their investment capacity in marketing, technology, and staff expansion.
3. **Leadership Structure**: The firm lacked a clearly defined leadership structure and needed to streamline decision-making processes.

Strategies Implemented

1. Innovative Service Offerings

Recognizing the need for innovation in the financial consulting industry, Dr. Chagadama and Dr. Luamba pursued the following strategies:

- **Digital Transformation**: The firm invested in digital tools to improve client interactions, automate processes, and enhance operational efficiency.
- **Tailored Solutions**: Star Light Consulting developed customized financial solutions for clients, addressing their unique needs and goals.
- **Educational Workshops**: They organized financial literacy workshops and webinars, fostering client engagement and empowerment.

2. Organizational Restructuring

To establish a more efficient organizational structure, the founders implemented the following strategies:

- **Leadership Roles**: Dr. Chagadama assumed the Chief Executive Officer (CEO) role, overseeing strategic planning and external relations, while Dr. Luamba took on the role of Chief Operating Officer (COO), focusing on operational efficiency and client services.
- **Team Expansion**: As the firm grew, they recruited additional consultants and support staff, each contributing to specific aspects of the company's growth.

- **Workflow Optimization**: Star Light Consulting LLC redesigned workflows and processes, reducing bottlenecks and improving client service delivery.

3. Marketing and Branding

To increase visibility and attract clients, the founders executed a comprehensive marketing strategy:

- **Online Presence**: The firm revamped its website, adopted Search Engine Optimization (SEO) strategies, and maintained an active presence on social media platforms.
- **Client Testimonials**: Encouraging satisfied clients to provide testimonials and referrals helped build trust and credibility.
- **Networking**: Dr. Chagadama and Dr. Luamba actively participated in industry conferences, workshops, and local business events, building valuable connections and partnerships.

Results Achieved

The strategies implemented by Star Light Consulting LLC produced impressive outcomes:

- **Increased Visibility**: The firm's online presence and targeted marketing efforts enhanced visibility and grew its client base in the DMV area.
- **Profitability**: Innovative service offerings, streamlined operations, and a client-centric approach contributed to improved profitability.
- **Viability**: A well-structured organization and sound leadership management enhanced the firm's long-term viability.
- **Client Satisfaction**: Star Light Consulting's commitment to personalized service and financial education fostered client satisfaction and loyalty.

Star Light Consulting LLC's inspiring journey demonstrates how innovation, a robust organizational structure, and effective leadership management can lead a small, minority-owned consulting business to achieve remarkable success[11]. By embracing change, leveraging digital tools, and fostering a client-centric approach, Dr. Chagadama and Dr. Luamba increased their firm's visibility and profitability, and they secured the company's long-term viability in the competitive financial consulting industry. This case study inspires small

[11] Star Light Consulting LLC. (2024). *About Our Firm*. Retrieved from https://gobrightstar.com/.

businesses seeking to thrive through innovation and sound management practices, regardless of their initial challenges.

1.8 Exercise: Quiz to assess knowledge of Chapter 1.

1. What is the primary purpose of an organization?
    a) To generate profits
    b) To provide employment
    c) To achieve common goals and objectives
    d) To reduce costs
2. Which of the following is NOT a type of organization?
    a) Corporation
    b) Partnership
    c) Volunteer organization.
    d) Individual
3. When we refer to the "size" of an organization, what are we typically measuring?
    a) The number of employees or members
    b) The physical dimensions of the office space
    c) The revenue generated.
    d) The age of the organization
4. Why is effective management important for an organization?
    a) To increase bureaucracy
    b) To complicate decision-making
    c) To achieve its goals and objectives efficiently
    d) To discourage employee involvement
5. What are the primary resources an organization requires for its operation?
    a) Office furniture and decorations
    b) A solid social media presence
    c) Financial capital, human resources, and physical assets
    d) Company logo and branding
6. What is the purpose of an organization's structure and design?
    a) To create chaos and confusion

b) To maximize employee autonomy
c) To facilitate coordination and efficient operations
d) To discourage collaboration

7. What are the most known types of organizations?
   a) Profits
   b) Nonprofits
   c) Privates
   d) Both Profits and nonprofits
8. The three main categories of organizations based on size are:
   a) Small, middle-sized, and large
   b) Public and private
   c) Profit and nonprofit.
   d) All the above
9. Effective knowledge management in an organization leads to the following:
   a) Increased competition with other organizations
   b) Reduced employee satisfaction
   c) Enhanced decision-making and innovation
   d) Greater focus on routine tasks
10. Which aspect of organizational culture represents the shared beliefs and values guiding employee behavior?
   a) Mission statement
   b) Vision statement
   c) Code of ethics
   d) Corporate values

1.9 Responses to the Quiz and Explanations of Correct Answers

1. Response C:

The primary value of an organization is to achieve common goals and objectives because this shared purpose brings individuals within the organization together and provides direction and focus for their collective efforts. The organization's primary purpose is to define its objective and lead to improved performance, motivation, and effectiveness, ultimately contributing to its success and sustainability.

2. Response D:

An individual cannot be considered an organization primarily because of the fundamental differences in structure, purpose, and functions between an individual and an organization. Individuals can be members or employees of organizations, but they are not equivalent to the complex entities that organizations represent.

3. Response A:

Having many employees provides insights into the organization's capacity and capability to reach its goals. Measuring the number of employees or members is also a practical and informative way to assess the size and scope of an organization, as it provides insights into various aspects of the organization's operations, impact, and strategic considerations.

4. Response C:

Effective management is essential for managers to achieve their goals and objectives efficiently. Also, it provides a clear sense of direction, focusing efforts on the most important tasks and priorities. Effective management is the driving force that enables an organization to set, pursue, and achieve its goals and objectives efficiently. Moreover, effective management provides the structure, leadership, and strategic direction necessary for success, ensuring that the organization remains adaptable, responsive, and focused on delivering results.

5. Response C:

Financial capital, human resources, and physical assets are considered principal resources of an organization because they are fundamental to its operations and ability to achieve its goals and objectives. These resources work in synergy and play critical roles in the success and sustainability of any organization. Financial capital enables an organization to buy equipment and hire skilled employees, and these employees, in turn, use their knowledge and expertise to manage and optimize physical assets. All three resources are integral to strategic decision-making, investment, and resource allocation, ultimately driving an organization's success and ability to achieve its goals and objectives.

6. Response C:

An organization's structure and design primarily aim to create an environment that promotes coordination, collaboration, and efficiency in its operations. This allows the organization to work cohesively toward its goals, adapt to changing circumstances, and maximize its effectiveness and performance.

7. Response D.

Organizations are mainly categorized into two categories: Profit and nonprofit organizations. Profit organizations focus on maximizing benefits or profits for their owners, while nonprofit organizations focus on serving people in society without making profits.

8. Answer A.

While "small," "middle-sized," and "large" are common general categories to describe organizations based on the size of the organization. Moreover, it's important to note that these terms can vary depending on context, industry, and location. There are no universally defined thresholds that categorize organizations into these size categories. The size classification can differ significantly between countries, industries, and sectors.

For instance, a "small" business in one industry may be considered a "medium-sized" business in another based on the number of employees, revenue, or assets. Government agencies and industry associations often provide specific criteria for defining the size of organizations within their sectors.

9. Response C.

Effective knowledge management contributes to more informed and efficient decision-making by providing easy access to information, reducing inefficiencies, and promoting learning from past experiences. Additionally, it fosters innovation by creating a culture of collaboration, knowledge sharing, and continuous improvement. As a result, organizations that invest in knowledge management are better positioned to adapt to changing circumstances, remain competitive, and drive innovation in their respective industries.

10. Response D.

Corporate values are a cornerstone of organizational culture and a compass for employee behavior, decision-making, and interactions. They help shape the organization's character and influence its relationships with employees, customers, and the broader community. Therefore, organizations often place great importance on defining, promoting, and upholding their corporate values.

Chapter 2

Statistics in Business Management

2.1 Introduction

In modern organizations' dynamic and data-driven landscape, statistics has emerged as a fundamental support in decision-making, resource allocation, and strategic planning. Statistics, the science of collecting, analyzing, interpreting, and presenting data, is a powerful tool that empowers organizations to gain valuable insights from information and make informed choices[12]. From multinational corporations to nonprofit entities, statistics has become an indispensable asset for organizations seeking to optimize performance, navigate uncertainties, and achieve their objectives precisely.

In this introduction, we delve into statistics' pivotal role in organizations, exploring its applications, benefits, and impact on various management aspects. Whether it's understanding market trends, evaluating employee performance, assessing financial risks, or measuring the effectiveness of programs, statistics provides a rigorous and objective approach to unlocking the potential within vast datasets. By embracing statistical methods and tools, organizations can harness the power of data to transform challenges into opportunities and drive success in an increasingly data-centric world.

Join us as we explore how statistics empowers organizations to make strategic decisions, uncover hidden patterns, and stay ahead of the curve. From the boardrooms to the frontlines, statistics shape how organizations operate, innovate, and adapt in an ever-evolving business landscape. As we navigate the complexities and possibilities of the statistical realm, we will discover how this discipline has become an indispensable asset for organizations striving for efficiency, growth, and sustainable success.

[12] Privitera, G. J. (2023). *Statistics for the behavioral sciences*. Sage publications.

2.2 What is "Statistics"?

Statistics can be understood in two contexts: as a science and as data[13]. The difference between the two is:

2.2.1 Statistics as a Science

Statistics as a science refers to the academic discipline and field of study that deals with data collection, analysis, interpretation, presentation, and organization. It is a branch of mathematics integral to various scientific, social, and business research endeavors. As a science, statistics involves developing and applying mathematical methods and techniques to draw inferences from data and make data-driven decisions.

Statistical science encompasses various subfields, including descriptive statistics, inferential statistics, probability theory, statistical modeling, and experimental design. Researchers and statisticians use statistical methods to analyze data, identify patterns, test hypotheses, and conclude populations based on samples.

2.2.2 Statistics as Data

Statistics as data refers to numerical information collected from observations, experiments, surveys, or any other data-gathering process.[14] In this context, statistics represent a collection of numbers, facts, figures, or values that describe different aspects of a specific phenomenon or population. These data points may include quantitative measurements, categorical attributes, or other information relevant to the research or analysis.

For example, when researchers conduct surveys to gather information about people's preferences for a particular product, the responses and data collected from the study are considered statistical data. Similarly, the measured outcomes and variables are treated as statistics as data in an experimental study.

In summary, the difference between statistics as a science and statistics as data lies in their respective meanings and contexts. Statistics as a science pertains to the systematic study and application of mathematical techniques to analyze and interpret data, while statistics as data refers to the actual numerical information

---

[13] Zapata-Cardona, L., & Martínez-Castro, C. A. (2023). Statistical modeling in teacher education. *Mathematical Thinking and Learning*, *25*(1), 64-78.

[14] Oluwafemi, E. J., & Otu, B. D. (2023). Skills for collecting research data, analytical skills, and lecturer job effectiveness at Nigerian universities. *Kabale University Interdisciplinary Research Journal, 2*(1), 51-63.

collected from observations and experiments, which is used as input for statistical analysis and decision-making.

2.3 Importance of Statistics

As a branch of mathematics, statistics deals with data collection, analysis, interpretation, presentation, and organization. It involves using quantitative techniques to draw meaningful insights from data and make informed decisions based on evidence. In both profit and nonprofit, statistics plays a crucial role in various ways:

1. Data Collection and Analysis

Statistics helps organizations collect data from various sources, such as market research, customer feedback, financial records, and operational processes. Through data analysis, patterns, trends, and relationships within the data can be identified, providing valuable information for decision-making.[15]

Example: Opinion polling using statistical methods, such as calculating percentages, means, or medians, to summarize the responses. Based on the sample data, confidence intervals and hypothesis tests may be used to make inferences about the entire population's opinions.

2. Market Research and Customer Insights

Understanding customer preferences, market trends, and demand patterns is essential for product development, pricing strategies, and marketing campaigns, especially in for-profit organizations. Statistics aids in analyzing market data and customer feedback to gain valuable insights.

Example: Market research and customer insights may help to understand consumer behavior, preferences, social media engagement, and market trends.

3. Performance Measurement

Statistics enables organizations to measure and evaluate their performance, both in terms of financial metrics and operational efficiency. Key performance

[15] Agarwal, S. A., Chauhan, N. K. S., & Ravikumar, S. (2024). *Basic Concepts of Research Methodology & Statistics*. Academic Guru Publishing House.

indicators (KPIs) can be tracked and analyzed, helping organizations identify strengths and weaknesses and make data-driven improvements.

Example: In an economic model, R-squared helps you understand how well the chosen independent variables (e.g., GDP, inflation, unemployment) explain variations in the stock market's performance.

4. Risk Assessment and Management

Businesses must assess investment risks, market changes, and operational decisions. Statistical techniques like probability and regression analysis help assess potential risks and develop risk management strategies.

Example: Collecting data on various attributes of loan applicants, such as income, credit score, employment history, and outstanding debts, will help to identify, analyze, and mitigate potential risks associated with data analysis or decision-making processes.

5. Resource Allocation

Both for-profit and nonprofit organizations have limited resources. Statistics assists in optimizing resource allocation through analyzing data on costs, revenues, and resource utilization, allowing for efficient distribution of funds and efforts.

Example: Allocating required budgets to different projects based on their priorities, expected impact, and resource requirements is strategic for a better resource allocation strategy.

6. Forecasting and Planning

Statistics enables organizations to make informed predictions and forecasts for future planning.

Example: Sales forecasts help businesses anticipate demand and plan production accordingly, while nonprofits can forecast funding needs for their projects.

7. Evidence-Based Decision-Making

Data-driven decision-making is becoming increasingly essential in both the profit and nonprofit sectors. Statistics provides a systematic approach to analyzing data objectively, reducing biases, and improving the quality of decisions.

Example: Collecting or gathering relevant data can help to make informed decisions such as:

- Population demographics in the city.
- Economic indicators like income levels and employment rates.
- Competitor locations and market share.
- Consumer behavior data in potential store locations.
- Historical sales data from existing stores, etc.

8. Program Evaluation

Nonprofit organizations often use statistics to evaluate the effectiveness and impact of their programs and initiatives. They can analyze relevant data to assess whether their efforts achieve the desired outcomes and adjust strategies accordingly.

Example: Identifying the key metrics and outcomes that will be used to evaluate the program's success. In this case, relevant metrics might include:

- Smoking cessation rates before and after the program.
- Changes in knowledge and attitudes related to smoking.
- Health outcomes like lung function and incidence of smoking-related diseases. Etc.

9. Compliance and Reporting

Statistics is instrumental in meeting regulatory requirements and financial reporting standards. Accurate data analysis ensures that organizations maintain compliance with legal and industry norms.

Example: Using statistical sampling technique to select a representative sample for periodic audits and reviews to ensure that the bank's compliance processes are effective and current.

10. Continuous Improvement

By regularly analyzing performance data, organizations can identify areas for improvement and implement targeted strategies to enhance efficiency, productivity, and overall performance.

Example: Implementing ongoing monitoring and evaluation to assess the program's long-term impact and make necessary adjustments.

2.4 Types of Statistics

As a science, statistics encompasses various branches and types catering to data analysis and inference. Data can be grouped or ungrouped. Ungrouped and grouped frequency distributions are two ways to organize and present data in statistics, mainly when dealing with large datasets[16].

They differ in how they handle data values and their associated frequencies. Here's a comparison of the two:

Ungrouped Frequency Distribution:

Individual Data Point: In an ungrouped frequency distribution, each unique data point is listed along with its frequency. It is suitable for relatively small datasets with few distinct values.[17]

Presentation: Data is presented as a list or table with two columns: one for data values (individual observations) and another for their respective frequencies.

Example

Data Value	Frequency
10	4
15	3
20	5
25	2
30	3

Granularity: Ungrouped distributions provide a detailed view of the data, showing the exact values and frequencies.

Suitability: It is typically used when there are relatively few unique data points or when the granularity of the data needs to be maintained.

[16] Green, S. B., & Salkind, N. J. (2017). *Using SPSS for Windows and Macintosh: Analyzing and understanding data* (8th ed.). Upper Saddle River, NJ: Pearson.
[17] Rivera, R. (2020). *Principles of managerial statistics and data science*. John Wiley & Sons.

Grouped Frequency Distribution

Data Intervals or Classes: In a grouped frequency distribution, data values are grouped into intervals or classes, and the frequencies within these intervals are counted. It is suitable for datasets with an extensive range of values.

Presentation: Data is presented as a table with two columns: one for data intervals (classes or bins) and another for their respective frequencies.

Granularity: Grouped distributions provide a more compact representation of data, making it easier to analyze and visualize large datasets.

Example:

Data Interval	**Frequency**
10-15	2
15-20	3
20-25	3
25-30	5
30-35	4

Suitability: It is used when dealing with datasets with a wide range of values or to simplify the data presentation. Grouping data into intervals can help identify patterns and trends without being overwhelmed by individual values.

In summary, choosing between ungrouped and grouped frequency distributions depends on the data's nature, size, and specific analysis or presentation goals. Ungrouped distributions maintain the granularity of the data, while grouped distributions provide a more condensed and manageable representation, making it easier to identify patterns and trends in large datasets.

Some Critical types of statistics are:

1. Descriptive Statistics

Descriptive statistics involve the summarization, organization, and meaningful presentation of data. Standard descriptive statistics are measures of:

(a) Measures of central tendency: mean, median, and mode.

(b) Measures of variability: range, variance, and standard deviation.[18]
(c) Graphical representations: histograms, bar charts, and scatter plots

to provide a clear and concise understanding of the data[19].

1.1. The Mean

Example 1: Customer Satisfaction Ratings

Suppose an organization conducts a customer satisfaction survey and collects ratings on a scale of 1 to 5 from 5 customers:

Customer	Satisfaction Rating (1-5)
1	4
2	3
3	5
4	1
5	3

Descriptive Statistics for Ungrouped Data:

To analyze the customer satisfaction survey data, you can calculate summary statistics and potentially create a visualization to gain insights into customer satisfaction. Here's how you can proceed:

Step 1: Calculate Summary Statistics

Calculate basic summary statistics to understand the central tendency and variability of the data:

- **Mean (Average)**: Sum of all ratings divided by the number of customers.

  Mean: (4 + 3 + 5 + 1 + 3) / 5 = 16 / 5 = 3.2

- **Median (Middle Value)**: The middle value when the ratings are ordered.

[18] Prasad, S. (2023). Basic Concepts in Research and Data Analysis. In *Elementary Statistical Methods* (pp. 1-36). Singapore: Springer Nature Singapore.
[19] Green, S. B., & Salkind, N. J. (2017). *Using SPSS for Windows and Macintosh: Analyzing and understanding data* (8th ed.). Upper Saddle River, NJ: Pearson.

Median: When ordered: 1, 3, 3, 4, 5; Middle value = 3

- **Mode (Most Frequent Value)**: The value that appears most frequently.

  Mode: The mode is 3 because it appears twice, more than any other rating.

- **Range (Max-Min)**: The difference between the highest and lowest ratings.

  Range: 5 (Max: 5 - Min: 1)

- **Standard Deviation (SD)**: It measures the spread or dispersion of the ratings.

Example 1: Standard Deviation Calculation Process

1. Calculate the squared difference between each rating and the mean.
2. Sum these squared differences.
3. Divide by (n-1), where n is the number of ratings.
4. Take the square root of the result.

Using these formulas: Standard Deviation of Ungrouped Data

$\sigma = \sqrt{(\sum x - \bar{x})2 / n}$), let's use an example of 4, 3, 5, 1, and 3 for a better understanding of Standard Deviation. As explained above, the mean is 16/5 =3.2.

1. Calculate squared differences: (4 - 3.2) ^2 = 0.64, (3 - 3.2) ^2 = 0.04, (5 - 3.2) ^2 = 3.24, (1 - 3.2)^2 = 4.84, (3 - 3.2)^2 = 0.04
2. Sum of squared differences: 0.64 + 0.04 + 3.24 + 4.84 + 0.04 = 8.8
3. Divide by (n-1): 8.8 / (5-1) = 2.2
4. Take the square root: $\sqrt{2.2} \approx 1.48$ (rounded to two decimal places)

So, the standard deviation is approximately 1.48.

Example 2: Customer Satisfaction Ratings by Age

Suppose a company conducted a customer satisfaction survey and collected the rating below on a scale of 1 to 5 from customers aged between 20 and 45 years.

Customer	Satisfaction Rating (1-5)
20-25	4
25-30	5
30-35	4
35-40	2
40-45	3

Descriptive Statistics for Grouped Data:

To analyze the customer satisfaction survey data, you can calculate summary statistics and potentially create a visualization to gain insights into customer satisfaction. Here's how you can proceed:

No	Classes	Frequencies ni	Center of Classes xi	Relative Frequencies fi=ni/∑ni	ni. xi	Cumulative frequencies Fc
1	20-25	4	22.5	0.22	90	4
2	25-30	5	27.5	0.28	140	9
3	30-35	4	32.5	0.22	132	13
4	35-40	2	37.5	0.11	76	15
5	40-45	3	42.5	0.17	136.5	18
		∑ni=18		∑fi=1.00	∑nixi=576.5	

- **Mean (Average)**: Sum of all weighted scores divided by the number of customers.

Average (Symbolized by X bar): $\bar{x} = \Sigma nixi/\Sigma ni = 576.5/18 = 32.02$

This indicates that the average customer satisfaction is around 4 with customers whose average age is 32.

- **Median:** the median value is a central value that divides the observed or grouped distribution into two parts with equal observations.

For grouped data, we calculate the median by linear interpolation:

- We divide the total number by 2 (n/2), and then we determine the median class, which corresponds to the cumulative numbers

Median is thus determined by the formula: Median =Li+a[n/2–Fc]/nimed

With Li: Lower limit of the middle class

Fc: Cumulative frequency descending to the lower limit of the median class

Nimed: Median workforce.

a: range of classes

Considering the previous example, the median=30+5(13-9)/4=30. The corresponding median age is 30 years, which corresponds to a level of satisfaction of 4, which is also very high and close to the high satisfaction rating of 5.

- **Mode:** If the observations are divided into classes, the mode is the midpoint of the class of the largest size, called modal class or dominant class.

The mode is calculated using the formula:

Mode = Li + a (fm–f1) /(fm–f1)+(fm–f2)

With: Li: Lower limit of the modal class

a: class amplitude

(fm-fl): Differences between the numbers of modal class and the previous class

(Fm-f2): Differences between the numbers of the modal class and the following class.

Considering the previous example, the mode is calculated as follows: 25+5(5-1)/ (5-1)+(5-1)

The mode is 27.5 years, which corresponds to the class with the most excellent customer satisfaction.

- **Range or Deviation (Max-Min)**: the difference between the upper and lower limit of the class intervals is 5.
- **Standard Deviation (σ):** it measures the deviation or dispersion of scores.

The formula determines the standard deviation of the grouped data.

$\sigma = \sqrt{(\sum ni(x-\bar{x})2 /n)}$.

Please note that the mean, median, and mode are position parameters. The differences are dispersion parameters. There are several other position and dispersion parameters. Still, considering their numbers, the complexity of calculations, and the content of this chapter is not a statistics course, we will spare you from their calculations. We invite you to refer to statistics courses or other statistical calculation software such as Excell, IBM SPSS, Minitab, Develve, XLSTAT, etc., which your statistician will recommend.

Step 2: Visualization

Histogram: It uses rectangular bars to show the frequency of data. You can create a histogram or bar chart to visualize the distribution of satisfaction ratings. This can help you see the distribution's shape and whether it's skewed or normally distributed. A distribution is symmetric or normal when mean=median=mode. Otherwise, it is asymmetrical, spread out to the left when mean<median<mode; and spread to the right when mean >median>mode. You can use a bar chart to create a histogram for the ungrouped frequency distribution of the ratings (1-5). Since this is an ungrouped frequency distribution, each rating is shown individually, and ratings are not grouped into intervals or classes. Here's how you can present the histogram:

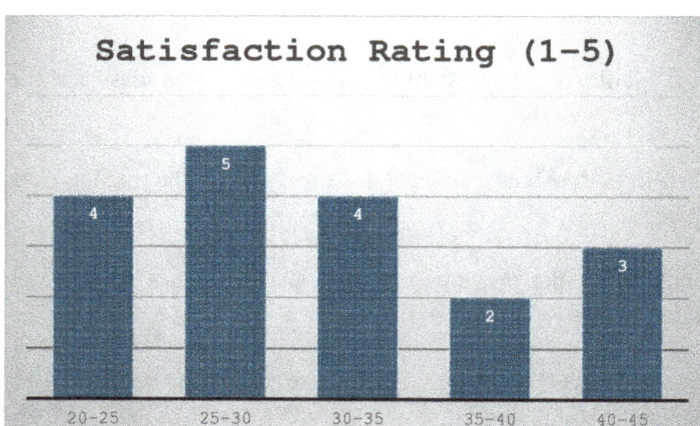

In this histogram, the Y-axis represents the customer satisfaction ratings (1 to 5), and the X-axis represents the count of customers who gave each rating. The bars show the frequency of each rating, with the height of each bar corresponding to the count of how customers assessed or rated their satisfaction.

These summary statistics and visualization provide insights into customer satisfaction, such as the average rating, most common rating, and the spread of ratings. However, with only five responses, be cautious about drawing definitive conclusions, as the sample size is relatively small.

Other Charts

Many charts exist; however, we will present a few of them for pedagogic reasons. For example:

1. PIE chart illustrating the distribution of satisfaction ratings. The PIE chart divides a circle into many sectors representing a proportion of the population.

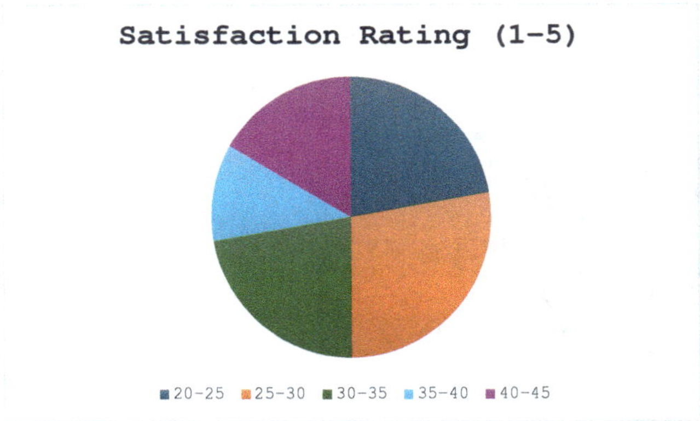

2. LINE Chart uses different lines to connect data points and show the overall trends for easy visualization and understanding of the phenomenon.

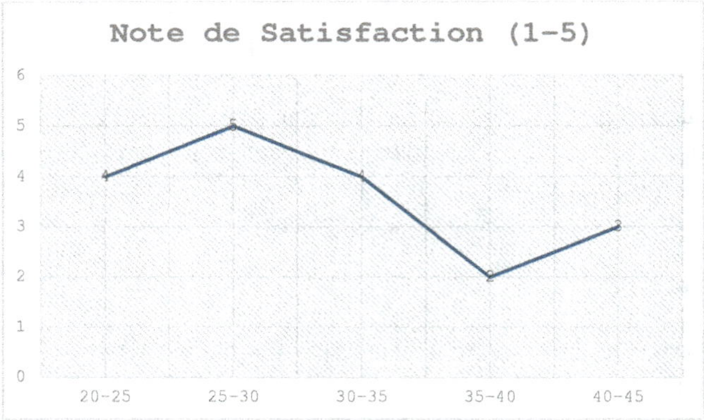

3. BAR: A bar chart is used to show and compare data of different sizes instead of the histogram, which shows the frequency of data. Both the bar chart and the histogram use column-based displays.

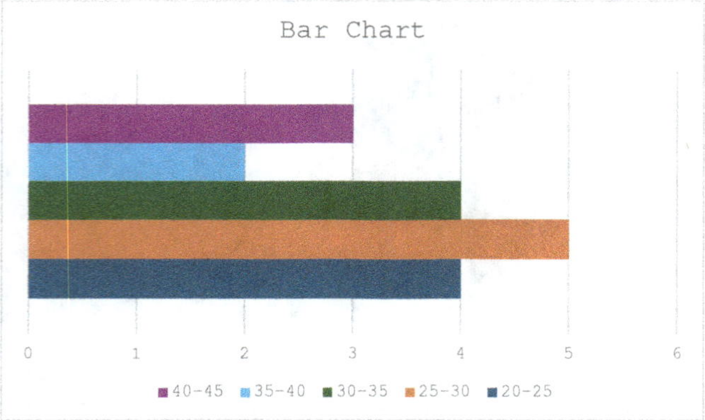

Example 3: Sales Performance by Region

Consider a multinational company that operates in different regions and collects sales data for the last quarter in its four regions:

Region	Ventes Totales $
Nord	50000
Sud	62000
Est	48000
Ouest	54000
Total	214000

Descriptive Statistics:

- Total Sales: $214000 (Sum of sales across all regions)
- Average Sales: $53500 (Total Sales / Number of regions)
- Maximum Sales: $62000 (The highest sales value among all regions)
- Minimum Sales: $50000 (The lowest sales value among all regions)

Bar showing the sales performance for each region.

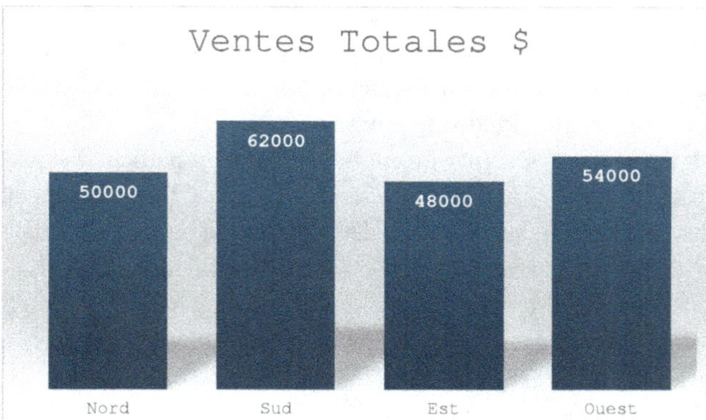

2. Inferential Statistics

   Inferential statistics are used to draw conclusions and make predictions about a population based on a sample of data. It involves hypothesis testing, confidence intervals, and regression analysis to infer relationships and inferences about the broader population from which the data was sampled.

Inferential statistics play a crucial role in business decision-making by drawing conclusions and making predictions based on sample data.

Examples of how inferential statistics may be used in business:

1. **Market Research and Customer Surveys:** Suppose a company wants to launch a new product and is interested in understanding the preferences of its target customers. They survey a randomly selected group of potential customers. Inferential statistics can be used to analyze the survey data and draw conclusions about the entire target population[20]. For example:

[20] Oh, D. M., & Pyrczak, F. (2023). *Making sense of statistics: A conceptual overview*. Routledge.

- **Confidence Intervals:** The company can calculate a confidence interval to estimate the range within which a certain percentage of customers will likely have a particular preference. This helps the company understand the potential demand for the new product.
- **Hypothesis Testing:** The company might have hypotheses about specific product features that would make it more appealing. They can use hypothesis testing to determine whether a statistically significant difference exists between certain groups' preferences, helping them decide which features to prioritize.

2. **Financial Analysis and Investment Decisions:** Inferential statistics can aid in making informed investment decisions and assessing financial performance. Consider the following scenario:
   - **Stock Price Analysis:** Investment firms analyze a particular stock's historical returns. They use inferential statistics to calculate the stock's mean return and standard deviation based on historical data. With this information, they can construct confidence intervals to estimate the likely range of future returns. Additionally, they might perform hypothesis testing to determine if the stock's performance is significantly different from a benchmark index.
   - **Portfolio Diversification:** A financial advisor helps clients build an investment portfolio. Based on historical data, inferential statistics can analyze the correlations between asset classes. By understanding the relationships between various assets, the advisor can recommend an optimal mix of investments that balances risk and return.

In both examples, inferential statistics enables businesses to make informed decisions by leveraging sample data to draw conclusions about larger populations or to assess relationships and patterns within data sets.

3. Probability Theory

Probability is a fundamental concept in statistics. It deals with the likelihood of different events occurring and is crucial in making predictions and understanding uncertainty. Probability theory is used in various statistical methods, such as Bayesian statistics and decision theory.

Examples:

Here are two examples of probability theories applied in business:

1. **Monte Carlo Simulation for Risk Analysis:** In business decision-making, uncertainty and risk play a significant role. Monte Carlo simulation is a probabilistic technique that uses random sampling to model the potential outcomes of a decision or project under various uncertain conditions. This method is widely used for financial forecasting, project management, and investment analysis. For instance, a company might use Monte Carlo simulation to assess a new product launch's potential returns and risks by considering variables such as market demand, production costs, and pricing. By running thousands of simulations, businesses can make more informed decisions based on the distribution of possible outcomes and their associated probabilities.
2. **Bayesian Inference for Marketing Campaigns:** Bayesian inference is a statistical method that updates beliefs or predictions based on new evidence. In business, Bayesian techniques are used in various ways, such as in marketing campaigns [1]. When a company launches a marketing campaign, it often starts with a prior belief about its effectiveness (e.g., a specific conversion rate).

   As the campaign progresses, new data is collected, and Bayesian inference is used to update the initial belief with the actual results observed during the campaign. This allows businesses to continuously refine their campaign performance estimates, allocate resources more effectively, and adjust based on real-time data.

These two examples highlight how probability theories can help businesses make better decisions by incorporating uncertainty, risk, and evolving information into their strategies and operations.

1. **Hypothesis Testing and A/B Testing:** A typical application of probability theory and statistics in business is hypothesis testing, particularly in the context of A/B testing for optimizing marketing strategies or product designs. When a company wants to determine whether a change (such as a new website layout, a different pricing strategy, or a revised marketing message) leads to a significant improvement, it conducts an A/B test. In this scenario, probability theory helps to assess the likelihood that the observed differences in outcomes (e.g., conversion rates, sales) between the control group (A) and the experimental group (B) are due to chance. Statistical techniques like t-tests or chi-square tests help quantify the significance level, allowing businesses to make informed decisions about adopting or rejecting the proposed change based on the observed data[1].

2. **Regression Analysis for Demand Forecasting:** Another application of probability theory and statistics in business is regression analysis for demand forecasting. Companies often must predict future sales or demand for their products or services. Regression analysis helps identify and quantify relationships between variables influencing the market, such as price, advertising expenditure, seasonality, and economic indicators. By applying probability distributions to the regression coefficients and error terms, businesses can estimate the range of possible outcomes for future demand and make more accurate predictions. This aids in inventory management, production planning, and resource allocation[21].

These examples demonstrate how probability theories and statistical techniques enable businesses to analyze data, make evidence-based decisions, and optimize their operations and strategies.

4. Biostatistics

Biostatistics is a specialized branch of statistics that focuses on the design and analysis of data in biology, medicine, public health, and related fields. It is critical in clinical trials, epidemiological studies, and medical research.[22]

Here are two examples of biostatistics applications:

1. **Clinical Trials and Experimental Design:** Biostatistics is crucial in designing and analyzing clinical trials, which are essential for evaluating the safety and efficacy of new medical treatments, drugs, or interventions. Biostatisticians help develop practices with appropriate sample sizes, randomization techniques, and control groups to ensure valid and reliable results. They also apply statistical methods to analyze the data collected during the trials, determining whether the observed effects are statistically significant and guiding decisions about the potential approval or adoption of the new treatment. Biostatistics ensures that clinical trials adhere to rigorous scientific standards and ethical considerations.
2. **Epidemiological Studies and Public Health Analysis:** Biostatistics is integral to epidemiology, the study of patterns, causes, and effects of diseases in populations. Biostatisticians analyze data from epidemiological

---

[21] Kaplan, D. (2023). *Bayesian statistics for the social sciences.* Guilford Publications.
[22] Kolassa, S., Rostami-Tabar, B., & Siemsen, E. (2023). *Demand forecasting for executives and professionals.* CRC Press.

studies to identify trends, risk factors, and associations between variables. For example, they might explore data from a cohort study to assess the relationship between smoking and lung cancer or use case-control studies to investigate outbreaks of infectious diseases. Biostatistics helps quantify the strength of associations, control for confounding variables, and estimate measures such as relative risks and odds ratios. These findings inform public health policies, interventions, and preventive measures to improve population health.

In both examples, biostatistics is used to collect, analyze, and interpret data in biology and healthcare, contributing to advancements in medical research, patient care, and public health strategies.

5. Econometrics

Econometrics applies statistical methods to economic data to model and analyze economic or financial relationships. It forecasts economic trends, evaluates policy effects, and understands economic behavior.

Here are two examples of statistics used in econometrics:

1. **Regression Analysis for Demand Estimation:** Econometrics often employs regression analysis to estimate and quantify relationships between economic variables. For instance, a company might use regression analysis to assess how changes in price, income, and other factors affect the demand for their product. By collecting data on historical sales, prices, and other relevant variables, economists can build a regression model that helps predict how changes in these factors will impact future demand. This information is crucial for businesses to make pricing decisions, allocate resources effectively, and plan production levels.
2. **Time Series Analysis for Economic Forecasting:** Time series analysis is a statistical technique used in econometrics to analyze and forecast economic data that evolves, such as stock prices, GDP, or unemployment rates. Time series analysis deals with data collected over time and aims to identify patterns, trends, and seasonality in the data. It is commonly used in financial forecasting, economic modeling, and environmental monitoring.

   Econometricians use Autoregressive Integrated Moving Average (ARIMA) models to identify patterns, trends, and seasonality in time series data. These models can then make short-term and long-term forecasts, helping policymakers, businesses, and investors anticipate economic conditions and make informed decisions. Time series analysis is also used to assess the impact of financial policies and external shocks on various economic indicators[23].

In both examples, statistics is a fundamental tool in econometrics, helping economists analyze data, build models, and draw meaningful insights to understand better and predict economic phenomena.

6. Multivariate Statistics

Multivariate statistics involves the simultaneous analysis of datasets with multiple variables. It includes techniques like factor analysis, Principal Component Analysis (PCA), and cluster analysis to explore relationships between variables.

Examples of multivariate statistics applications:

1. **Principal Component Analysis (PCA) for Dimensionality Reduction:** PCA is a widely used multivariate statistical technique that aims to reduce the dimensionality of a dataset while preserving as much of its variability as possible. In finance, PCA can be applied to a portfolio of stocks to identify the key underlying factors that drive their returns. By reducing the original dataset's dimensions, analysts can focus on the most significant components, making it easier to interpret and model the relationships between different assets. This helps in portfolio optimization, risk management, and identifying sources of risk and return.
2. **Cluster Analysis for Market Segmentation:** Cluster analysis is a multivariate technique used to group similar data points based on their attributes. In marketing, businesses often use cluster analysis to segment their customer base into distinct groups with similar purchasing behavior, preferences, or demographics. Companies can identify target segments and tailor their marketing strategies to each group's needs by analyzing multivariate data like customer age, income, purchase history, and preferences. This allows for more effective marketing campaigns, personalized offers, and improved customer satisfaction.

[23] Green, S. B., & Salkind, N. J. (2017). *Using SPSS for Windows and Macintosh: Analyzing and understanding data* (8th ed.). Upper Saddle River, NJ: Pearson.

These examples show how multivariate statistics enables researchers and businesses to extract meaningful patterns, reduce complexity, and make informed decisions based on data that involves multiple variables.

7. Nonparametric Statistics

Nonparametric statistics do not rely on specific assumptions about the underlying data distribution. It is useful when data does not meet the assumptions of traditional parametric tests, offering robust alternatives.

Examples of nonparametric statistics applications:

1. **Rank Sum Test (Mann-Whitney U Test):** The Mann-Whitney U test is a nonparametric method used to compare two independent groups and determine whether their distributions differ significantly. This test is beneficial when the assumptions of parametric tests like the t-test are not met (e.g., when the data is not normally distributed or when the variances are unequal). For example, in a clinical trial, researchers might use the Mann-Whitney U test to compare the effectiveness of two treatments by analyzing the ranks of patients' responses rather than assuming specific distributional properties of the data.
2. **Spearman's Rank Correlation Coefficient:** Spearman's rank correlation coefficient is a nonparametric measure of the strength and direction of a monotonic relationship between two variables. Unlike Pearson's correlation coefficient, which assumes a linear relationship, Spearman's coefficient does not require the data to follow a specific distribution or have a linear association. This makes it suitable for analyzing ordinal or ranked data. For instance, in social sciences, researchers might use Spearman's rank correlation to assess the relationship between the rankings of individuals' socioeconomic status and their levels of education without assuming a linear trend between the variables.

These examples demonstrate the use of nonparametric statistics when the assumptions of traditional parametric methods are not met or when dealing with data that doesn't adhere to specific distributional requirements.

8. Quality Control and Six Sigma

Quality control and Six Sigma use statistical techniques to monitor and improve the quality of products and processes in manufacturing and service industries.

Examples:

1. **Manufacturing Defect Reduction using Control Charts (Quality Control):** In a manufacturing setting, control charts are commonly used for quality control. Consider a company that produces electronic components such as microchips. They implement control charts to monitor the thickness of each microchip. The company sets upper and lower control limits based on historical data and specifications. As new microchips are manufactured, samples are taken and measured. Any measurements that fall outside the control limits trigger an alert, indicating a potential issue in the manufacturing process. This early detection allows the company to investigate and correct the problem before producing a large batch of defective products. Control charts help maintain consistent product quality by identifying and addressing variations in the production process.
2. **Reducing Customer Complaints in a Call Center (Six Sigma):** Imagine a call center that receives customer complaints about long wait times and unresolved issues. To address this, the call center applies the Six Sigma methodology. They define the problem, measuring key metrics such as average wait time and customer satisfaction scores. Then, they analyze the root causes of the issues, using tools like Pareto charts to identify the most common reasons for complaints. Based on the analysis, they implement process improvements such as streamlining call routing, optimizing staff schedules, and providing additional training to agents. After implementing changes, the call center monitors the metrics to ensure sustained improvements. By systematically applying Six Sigma principles and statistical techniques, the call center reduces customer complaints, enhances service quality, and increases customer satisfaction.[24]

In these examples, statistical techniques are central to quality control and Six Sigma methodologies, enabling businesses to identify areas for improvement, make data-driven decisions, and enhance the overall quality of products and services. Each type of statistic serves a unique purpose and is applied in specific contexts to extract meaningful insights and support decision-making in various fields of study and industries.

2.5 Chapter Summary

Statistics plays a crucial role in both types of organizations. It aids in collecting, analyzing, and interpreting data, providing valuable insights into market trends, consumer behavior, and operational performance. By harnessing statistical data,

[24] Black, K. (2023). *Business statistics: for contemporary decision making*. John Wiley & Sons.

organizations can make informed decisions about product development, market expansion, resource allocation, and risk assessment. For-profit organizations use statistics to identify growth opportunities, optimize production processes, and enhance customer experiences. In contrast, nonprofit organizations use it to evaluate the impact of their initiatives, plan strategic campaigns, and allocate resources efficiently. In today's data-driven world, organizations that harness the power of statistics are better equipped to thrive and succeed in their respective sectors.

2.6 Case Study: Leveraging Statistics for Informed Decision-Making at Organization ABC Manufacturing

Overview: ABC Manufacturing is a medium-sized manufacturing company specializing in consumer electronics. To stay competitive in a rapidly evolving market, ABC Manufacturing recognizes the critical role of statistics as a source of data and a scientific discipline in optimizing its operations and decision-making processes.

Role of Statistics as Data: ABC Manufacturing collects vast amounts of data throughout its operations, including production processes, quality control, sales, and customer feedback. These data points serve as valuable inputs for statistical analysis, enabling the company to gain insights into its performance, identify areas for improvement, and make informed decisions.

Role of Statistics as a Science: Statistics is a powerful scientific tool that ABC Manufacturing employs to extract meaningful insights from its data. The company applies statistical methods and techniques to analyze patterns, trends, correlations, and probabilities, which inform strategic choices and enhance efficiency.

Application of Descriptive Statistics: Descriptive statistics have dramatically improved management at ABC Manufacturing. They provide a clear snapshot of key performance indicators by summarizing and presenting data meaningfully.

Example: ABC Manufacturing uses descriptive statistics to monitor and improve production efficiency. They analyze the average production time per unit over different shifts and days of the week and summarize the data using mean, median, and standard deviation measures.

Graphical Representation: ABC Manufacturing employs a histogram to visualize the data and facilitate decision-making. The histogram displays the sales of production from 2019 to 2022.

Impact: ABC Manufacturing identified inefficiencies during specific shifts by analyzing and graphically presenting production time data using descriptive statistics. This insight prompted management to allocate resources more effectively, adjust staffing levels, and implement process improvements. As a result, production efficiency increased, reducing costs and improving product delivery times.

ABC Manufacturing's case exemplifies the dual role of statistics: as a source of data and a scientific discipline. The company improved its management processes by applying descriptive statistics and visualizing data through graphs, enhancing operational efficiency and ultimately contributing to its competitiveness in the consumer electronics market.[25]

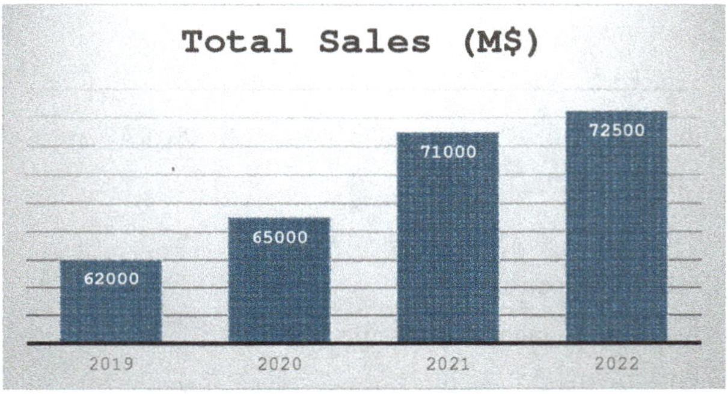

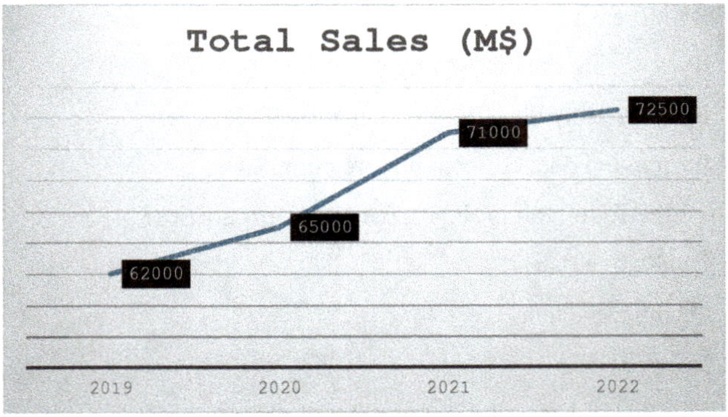

[25] ABC Assembly Inc. (2023). *We Are Electronic*. Retrieved from https://abcassembly.com/.

2.7 Quiz to Assess Knowledge of Chapter 2

1. What is the primary goal of statistics as a science?
    a) To manipulate data
    b) To collect data
    c) To summarize and analyze data
    d) To interpret data
2. In the context of statistics, what is the term "descriptive statistics" used for?
    a) Predicting future trends
    b) Summarizing and describing data
    c) Designing experiments
    d) Analyzing data using regression models
3. How can data analytics benefit a business or organization?
    a) By increasing data storage costs
    b) By reducing data collection efforts
    c) By improving decision-making and efficiency
    d) By making data collection more complex
4. Which of the following is NOT a data type in statistics?
    a) Qualitative data
    b) Quantitative data
    c) Nominal data
    d) Emotional data
5. What is the primary role of inferential statistics?
    a) To describe data
    b) To make predictions and inferences about populations
    c) To present data using graphs
    d) To manipulate data for visualization
6. Which of the following is a benefit of using data visualization in business or organizations?
    a) It adds complexity to data analysis.

b) It makes data more challenging to understand.

c) It simplifies complex data for more straightforward interpretation.

d) It increases data storage requirements.

7. What type of graph or diagram is typically used to show the distribution of a dataset?

   a) Line chart.

   b) Scatter plot.

   c) Histogram.

   d) Bar chart.

8. Which data type is categorical and cannot be ordered or ranked?

   a) Ordinal data

   b) Interval data

   c) Nominal data

   d) Ratio data

9. What is the primary purpose of a vertical bar graph or chart in data analysis?

   a) To display a time series of data

   b) To show the correlation between two variables

   c) To display and compare data.

   d) To compare different categories of data

10. What does the term "correlation" refer to in statistics?

    a) A measure of the strength and direction of the relationship between two variables

    b) A type of data visualization

    c) A statistical test for hypothesis testing

    d) A method for data collection

2.8 Answer to the Quiz and Explanation of Correct Answers

1. Answer C.

The primary goal of statistics in the organization is to provide a systematic and rigorous framework for summarizing and analyzing data, enabling managers to extract knowledge, make informed decisions, and better understand the business environment.

2. Answer B

Descriptive statistics serve as the foundation for statistical analysis and data interpretation. They allow organizational managers to gain initial insights, make data more understandable, and lay the groundwork for more advanced statistical techniques, making them an essential component of the statistical toolkit.

3. Answer C

Data analytics can benefit a business or organization by improving decision-making and efficiency. Data analytics empowers businesses and organizations to leverage their data for improved decision-making and operational efficiency. By extracting actionable insights from data, they can make more informed choices, allocate resources more effectively, and gain a competitive edge in their respective industries.

4. Answer D.

Emotional data is not considered a distinct data type because statistical analysis primarily involves objective, quantifiable, and measurable data. In statistics, data are typically categorized into the following types: Nominal, ordinal, interval, and ratio. In summary, emotional data is not a recognized type of data in statistics because it does not fit the standard categories of data typically analyzed using statistical techniques.

5. Answer B.

The primary role of inferential statistics is to make predictions and inferences about populations based on data collected from a sample of that population. This is because inferential statistics aims to conclude a larger group (the population) from a smaller, representative subset (the sample) of that group.

Moreover, Inferential statistics employs various techniques, including confidence intervals, hypothesis tests, regression analysis, and more, to provide a structured and systematic way to make predictions and inferences about populations while accounting for the inherent uncertainty associated with sampling. This is why making predictions and inferences about populations is the primary role of inferential statistics.

6. Answer C.

The benefit of using data visualization in business or organizations to simplify complex data for more straightforward interpretation is that visual representations of data can convey information more effectively than raw numbers and complex datasets. Data visualization makes it easier for individuals to comprehend the data, gain insights, and use it to make informed decisions, ultimately benefiting businesses and organizations in their data-driven endeavors.

7. Answer C

A histogram is typically used to show the distribution of a dataset because it provides a visual representation of the frequency or density of data points within specific intervals or "bins." This makes it particularly useful for visualizing the distribution of continuous data, such as measurements, scores, or values. Overall, histograms are a powerful tool for summarizing and visualizing data distributions, making them a fundamental component of exploratory data analysis and a valuable aid in data interpretation and decision-making in various fields, including statistics, data science, and research.

8. Answer C.

Nominal data cannot be ordered or ranked because it represents categories or labels with no inherent order or magnitude. In the hierarchy of data types, nominal data is the simplest and most basic form of categorical data. Nominal data is primarily used for classifying or categorizing data into different groups but does not allow for meaningful quantitative comparisons or rankings.

9. Answer C.

The primary purpose of a vertical bar graph or chart in data analysis is not necessarily to prioritize problems or causes in descending order; instead, it is to display and compare categorical data or values for different categories. Vertical bar charts, or bar graphs, are versatile and widely used for various purposes, including comparison, distribution, trends, frequency, and ranking.

10. Answer A.

In statistics, "correlation" refers to a measure that quantifies the strength and direction of the relationship between two or more variables. Correlation is used to assess how variables are related to each other. There are different types of correlation coefficients, but the most common one is the Pearson correlation coefficient (often denoted as "r"), which measures the linear relationship between two continuous variables.

Chapter 3

Accounting in Business Management

3.1 Introduction

In real business management, accounting is an indispensable pillar that provides a clear and comprehensive view of an organization's financial health and performance. As an intricate system of recording, analyzing, and interpreting financial transactions, accounting is the bedrock for informed decision-making, resource allocation, and strategic planning.[26] In Chapter 3 of this comprehensive guide on business management, we delve into the fundamental significance of accounting and its multifaceted applications in guiding organizations toward success and sustainability.

Amidst the complexities of modern business operations, accurate and reliable financial information forms the backbone of managerial decision-making. With precise and standardized methods, accounting offers insights into an organization's profitability, liquidity, solvency, and overall financial stability. Through financial statements, balance sheets, income statements, and cash flow reports, managers gain the essential tools to assess the organization's financial performance and identify areas for improvement.

This chapter explores the various facets of accounting in business management. We begin by uncovering the core principles and practices that underpin sound accounting methods, highlighting the importance of transparency, accuracy, and ethical standards. Furthermore, we examine the role of accounting in financial planning and budgeting, as managers rely on accurate financial data to set realistic goals, allocate resources, and adapt to changing market conditions.

Beyond financial reporting, we delve into cost accounting, understanding how organizations track and analyze costs to optimize profitability and make informed pricing decisions. The concepts of managerial accounting come to the forefront, where internal financial data aids managers in making day-to-day operational choices, optimizing production processes, and maximizing efficiency.

---

[26] Adebiyi, O. O. (2023). Exploring the impact of predictive analytics on accounting and auditing expertise: A Regression analysis of LinkedIn survey data. *Available at SSRN 4626506.*

Moreover, this chapter also touches upon the vital role of accounting in compliance and regulatory adherence. We explore the significance of following accounting standards, such as Generally Accepted Accounting Principles (GAAP) or International Financial Reporting Standards (IFRS), to ensure financial statements meet legal requirements and instill stakeholder confidence.

As we journey through Chapter 3, it becomes evident that accounting serves not merely as a record-keeping function but as a strategic tool that guides managers in understanding the financial implications of their decisions. From startups to multinational corporations, from nonprofit organizations to for-profit enterprises, accounting principles are a common language that facilitates effective communication and informed decision-making across all facets of business management.

Join us in this exploration of Chapter 3, where we unravel the nuances of accounting in business management. This discipline empowers managers to navigate challenges, seize opportunities, and lead their organizations toward sustainable growth and prosperity in an ever-evolving business landscape.

3.2 What is Accounting?

Accounting is the process of recording, summarizing, analyzing, and interpreting financial transactions and information of an organization. It systematically records all accounting activities, including revenues, expenses, assets, and liabilities. The primary purpose of accounting is to provide accurate and reliable financial data that can be used for decision-making, financial reporting, and overall management of the organization's resources.[27]

The role and importance of accounting in both profit and nonprofit organizations are significant and include the following:

1. Financial Reporting

   Accounting produces financial statements, such as the income statement, balance sheet, and cash flow statement, which offer a comprehensive overview of the organization's financial health. These reports are essential for internal management and external stakeholders, including investors, creditors, and donors.

[27] Kimmel, P. D., Weygandt, J. J., Kieso, D. E., Mitchell, J. E., Trenholm, B., Irvine, W., & Burnley, C. D. (2023). *Financial accounting: Tools for business decision making*. John Wiley & Sons.

2. Budgeting and Planning

   Accounting data serves as the foundation for creating budgets and financial plans. Organizations use historical financial information to project future income, expenses, and cash flows, allowing them to set realistic financial goals and make informed decisions.

3. Tax Compliance

   Proper accounting practices are crucial for fulfilling tax obligations. Accurate financial records enable organizations to calculate and report their tax liabilities, avoiding penalties and legal issues.

4. Performance Evaluation

   Accounting helps assess an organization's financial performance over time. By analyzing financial statements and key financial ratios, management can identify areas of strength and weakness, enabling them to take corrective actions if necessary.

5. Resource Allocation

   Profit and non-profit organizations must allocate resources efficiently using accounting data to provide insights into cost structures, revenue streams, and profitability and enable organizations to optimize their use of resources.

6. Decision-Making

   Sound financial information is essential for making strategic decisions. Accounting data provides the necessary financial analysis to evaluate potential opportunities and risks, whether launching a new product line, expanding operations, or initiating a new project.

7. Financial Stability

   For-profit organizations need accounting to gauge their financial stability and profitability. Nonprofits rely on accounting to ensure sufficient funds to fulfill their missions and serve their beneficiaries effectively.

8. Accountability and Transparency

   Proper accounting practices promote accountability and transparency within an organization. By maintaining accurate financial records, organizations can demonstrate responsible stewardship of resources to stakeholders and the public.

9. Investor and Donor Confidence

   Both profit and nonprofit organizations must instill confidence in their investors and donors. Transparent and well-maintained financial records foster trust and attract potential investors and donors.

10. Legal Compliance: Organizations must comply with various financial regulations and reporting standards. Accounting ensures that organizations meet these requirements, safeguarding them from legal and regulatory issues.

3.3 Who uses accounting data?

Internal and external users use accounting data to assess a business or organization's financial health, performance, and decision-making.[28] Here's how both groups utilize accounting data:

3.3.1 Internal Users:

1. Management: Internal users, especially at various levels, rely on accounting data to make informed decisions about resource allocation, budgeting, pricing strategies, cost control, and overall business operations. Financial statements and reports help managers monitor performance and guide strategic planning.
2. Employees: Employees within different departments use accounting information to understand the financial implications of their activities[29]. For example, production teams might use cost data to optimize manufacturing processes, while sales teams might use revenue and profit information to set sales targets and evaluate performance.

[28] Kimmel, P. D., Weygandt, J. J., Kieso, D. E., Mitchell, J. E., Trenholm, B., Irvine, W., & Burnley, C. D. (2023). Financial accounting: Tools for business decision making. John Wiley & Sons.
[29] Luamba, D. S., Chagadama, J., Blye, M. L., & James, K. C. The Impacts of Audit Transparency on Increasing Trust in Nonprofit Organizations.

3. Board of Directors: Board members use accounting data to assess the company's financial health, monitor management's performance, and make high-level decisions that impact the organization's direction.
4. Investors and Shareholders: Investors who own shares in a company use accounting data to evaluate the company's financial performance, growth potential, and risk before making investment decisions.

3.3.2 External Users:

1. Creditors and Lenders: Banks, financial institutions, and other creditors use accounting data to assess a company's creditworthiness and ability to repay loans. They analyze financial statements to make lending decisions and determine interest rates.
2. Investors: External investors, such as individuals, mutual funds, and institutional investors, use accounting data to evaluate investment opportunities, estimate potential returns, and assess the risks associated with investing in a particular company.
3. Government and Regulatory Agencies: Government agencies, such as tax authorities, use accounting data to ensure compliance with tax laws and regulations. Regulatory bodies may also require businesses to provide financial information to demonstrate adherence to industry-specific standards.
4. Suppliers and Vendors: Suppliers and vendors may analyze a company's financial statements to evaluate its ability to pay bills and fulfill contractual obligations.
5. Customers: In some cases, customers may review a company's financial information to assess its stability and ability to provide consistent products or services.

Internal and external users rely on accounting data to make a wide range of decisions that impact their interactions with the business, whether related to financial management, investment, lending, or strategic planning.

3.4 The Building Blocks of Accounting

The building blocks of accounting provide the foundation for accurate and consistent financial reporting. These building blocks include:

1. **Ethical Norms and Standards in Financial Reporting**: Ethical norms and standards are essential in accounting to ensure financial information's

accuracy, transparency, and integrity. Accountants must adhere to ethical principles such as honesty, objectivity, confidentiality, and professional competence. These norms guide accountants in making unbiased judgments and decisions while preparing and presenting financial statements.

2. **Accounting Principles (Generally Accepted Accounting Principles—GAAP):** Accounting principles are the fundamental guidelines governing how financial transactions and events should be recorded, reported, and interpreted. GAAP provides a standardized framework for financial reporting, ensuring consistency and comparability across organizations and industries.[30] Examples of accounting principles include the revenue recognition principle, the matching principle, and the historical cost principle.
3. **Assumptions:** Assumptions are foundational concepts that underlie the accounting process and financial reporting. They help accountants make realistic estimates and interpretations when dealing with uncertainties. Three critical assumptions in accounting are:
   - Going Concern Assumption: This assumption assumes that the business will continue to operate indefinitely. It allows accountants to value assets and liabilities based on their long-term use rather than immediate liquidation.
   - Consistency Assumption: This assumption requires that accounting methods and practices remain consistent over time, enabling meaningful comparisons of financial statements from one period to another.
   - Time-Period Assumption: This assumption divides the financial reporting process into specific time intervals (e.g., months, quarters, years), allowing businesses to provide regular and timely updates on their financial performance.

These building blocks collectively create a framework that guides accountants in recording and reporting financial information accurately and transparently. They help ensure that financial statements are reliable, comparable, and useful for various stakeholders' decision-making.

[30] Joshi, P., & India, U. (2023). Role of Financial Reporting Standards in Enhancing Transparency and Accountability: An Empirical Study.

3.5 The Basic Accounting Equation

The basic accounting equation, the fundamental accounting or balance sheet equation, serves as the foundation for double-entry bookkeeping and financial reporting. It is expressed as:

Assets = Liabilities + Stockholders' Equity[31]

Here's a breakdown of the components of the basic accounting equation:

1. **Assets:** Assets represent the economic resources owned or controlled by a business that have measurable value and provide future benefits. Assets can include tangible items like cash, inventory, equipment, and property and intangible assets like patents and trademarks.
2. **Liabilities are the obligations or debts** a business owes to external parties. They arise from past transactions or events and represent claims against the business's assets. Examples of liabilities include loans, accounts payable, and accrued expenses.
3. **Stockholders' Equity**: Also referred to as owner's equity or shareholders' equity, this represents the residual interest in the assets of a business after deducting liabilities. It reflects the owners' claims on the company's assets. Stockholders' equity includes common stock, retained earnings, and additional paid-in capital.
4. **Transaction Analysis**: Transaction analysis identifies and records the financial effects of business transactions on the accounting equation. Every business transaction affects at least two accounts, one debited and another credited. The total debits must always equal the total credits to maintain the balance in the accounting equation.

For example, if a company borrows $10,000 from a bank, the transaction analysis would involve increasing the "Cash" asset account by $10,000 (debit) and increasing the "Loan Payable" liability account by $10,000 (credit). This keeps the accounting equation in balance:

Assets ($10,000) = Liabilities ($10,000) + Stockholders' Equity (remains unchanged)

[31] Kasim, C., & Lobo, A. C. (2023). Stockholder's Equity. Available at SSRN 4511159.

The basic accounting equation is a fundamental accounting tool helping to ensure that a company's financial statements accurately reflect its financial position and performance.

3.6 Different Types of Accounting in Organizations

Accounting in organizations can be categorized into various types or categories, each serving a specific purpose and contributing to the overall financial management and reporting processes. Here are some of the main categories of accounting within an organization:

1. **Financial Accounting:** Financial accounting involves preparing and reporting an organization's financial statements for external stakeholders, such as investors, creditors, regulators, and the general public. These statements, including the balance sheet, income statement, and cash flow statement, provide a comprehensive overview of the company's financial performance and position.
2. **Managerial Accounting:** Managerial accounting provides internal managers with financial information for decision-making, planning, and control. This type of accounting includes cost accounting, budgeting, variance analysis, and performance measurement. It helps managers allocate resources efficiently, control costs, and make strategic decisions.
3. **Cost Accounting:** Cost accounting involves tracking and analyzing the costs incurred by an organization in producing goods or providing services. It helps determine the price of products, assess the profitability of different product lines, and make pricing decisions.
4. **Tax Accounting:** Tax accounting ensures compliance with tax laws and regulations. It involves calculating and reporting taxes payable, preparing tax returns, and staying updated on changes in tax laws to optimize the organization's tax position.
5. **Auditing:** Auditing involves examining an organization's financial records, transactions, and internal controls to assess their accuracy, completeness, and compliance with accounting standards and regulations. Independent auditors conduct external audits, while an organization's internal audit department drives internal audits.
6. **Forensic Accounting:** Forensic accounting combines accounting, investigative skills, and legal knowledge to uncover financial fraud, embezzlement, and other financial irregularities. Forensic accountants may be involved in legal proceedings and provide expert testimony in court.

7. **Government and Nonprofit Accounting:** Government and nonprofit organizations have specific accounting requirements due to their unique funding sources and reporting needs. These organizations often follow different accounting standards (such as Generally Accepted Accounting Principles - GAAP) tailored to their sector.
8. **International Accounting:** International accounting deals with accounting standards and practices globally, considering different countries' diverse accounting regulations and reporting requirements. Organizations with international operations must navigate variations in accounting rules and currencies.
9. **Sustainability Accounting:** Sustainability accounting, also known as environmental accounting or social accounting, focuses on measuring and reporting an organization's environmental and social impact. This includes tracking carbon emissions, energy consumption, social responsibility initiatives, and other non-financial performance metrics.
10. **Management Information Systems (MIS) Accounting:** MIS accounting involves utilizing technology and information systems to collect, process, and analyze financial data for decision-making and reporting purposes. It bridges the gap between accounting and information technology to improve efficiency and accuracy in financial operations.

These categories of accounting work together to ensure accurate financial reporting, effective decision-making, compliance with regulations, and the efficient allocation of resources within an organization.

3.7 Financial Statements Presentation

Financial statements are crucial documents that provide a comprehensive view of a company's financial performance, position, and cash flow over a specific period. Here's an overview of the mentioned financial statements:

1. **Income Statement**: Also known as the Profit and Loss statement (P&L), the income statement summarizes a company's revenues, expenses, and net income or net loss over a specific period (usually a fiscal quarter or year). It shows how much money the company earned from its operations and how much it spent to generate that revenue.[32]

[32] Aziz, F. (2023). *Beyond the Ledger: Enhancing Global Sustainability through Data-Driven Accounting Frameworks*. Farooq Aziz.

The formula is:

Net Income = Total Revenues - Total Expenses

The income statement helps stakeholders understand the company's profitability and assess its ability to generate profits.

2. **Retained Earnings Statement**: The retained earnings statement shows the changes in a company's retained earnings account over a specific period. Retained earnings represent the accumulated net profits or losses a company has retained for reinvestment in the business rather than distributing them as dividends. The statement starts with the beginning balance of retained earnings, adds net income, and subtracts dividends to calculate the ending retained earnings balance.

Ending Retained Earnings = Beginning Retained Earnings + Net Income - Dividends

This statement provides insights into how profits have been reinvested in the company over time.

3. **Balance Sheet:** The balance sheet, also called the statement of financial position, presents a snapshot of a company's financial position at a specific time. It lists the company's assets, liabilities, and stockholders' equity, following the basic accounting equation (Assets = Liabilities + Stockholders' Equity). The balance sheet helps stakeholders understand the company's financial health and the relationship between its resources (assets) and obligations (liabilities).
4. **Statement of Cash Flows**: The statement of cash flows provides information about a company's cash inflows and outflows during a specific period, categorized into operating, investing, and financing activities. It helps stakeholders understand how a company generates and uses its cash and ability to meet short-term and long-term obligations. The statement of cash flows is divided into three sections: operating activities, investing activities, and financing activities.

   Operating Activities:

   In accounting, operating activities refer to the cash flows directly related to the company's core business operations. These activities include revenue generation, day-to-day expenses, and changes in working capital.

Example: Star Light LLC Company sells $100,000 worth of products to its customers. The company also pays $50,000 to its suppliers for inventory purchases. Additionally, it collects $30,000 from its customers who previously bought goods on credit. Finally, it pays $20,000 to its employees as wages.

Cash received from customers: $100,000 (sales) + $30,000 (collections from accounts receivable) = $130,000

Cash paid to suppliers: $50,000 (inventory purchases)

Cash paid for wages: $20,000.

Net cash flow from operating activities: $130,000 - $50,000 - $20,000 = $60,000

Investing Activities:

Investing activities involve acquiring and disposing of long-term assets that are not considered part of the company's core operations. These activities include purchasing or selling Property, Plant, and Equipment (PP&E) and investments in securities of other companies.

Example: Star Light Consulting LLC purchases a new manufacturing facility for $200,000 and sells an old piece of machinery for $50,000. It also invests $100,000 in stocks of another company.

Cash paid for new manufacturing facility: $200,000.

Cash received from the sale of old machinery: $50,000.

Cash invested in stocks: $100,000.

Net cash flow from investing activities: ($200,000 + $100,000) - $50,000 = $250,000

Financing Activities:

Financing activities involve transactions with owners and creditors that affect the company's capital structure. These activities include issuing or repurchasing the company's stock, obtaining, or repaying loans, and paying dividends to shareholders.

Example: Star Light Consulting LLC Company issues $300,000 in bonds to finance its expansion, repays $50,000 of its outstanding loans, and pays $20,000 in dividends to its shareholders.

Cash received from issuing bonds: $300,000.

Cash paid for loan repayment: $50,000.

Cash paid for dividends: $20,000.

Net cash flow from financing activities: $300,000 - $50,000 - $20,000 = $230,000

These examples illustrate how cash flows are categorized into operating, investing, and financing activities in accounting, providing insights into how a company generates and utilizes its cash resources.

The statement of cash flows ensures that the company's reported net income on the income statement is reconciled with its actual cash flows.

These financial statements offer a comprehensive view of a company's financial performance, position, and cash flow, aiding investors, creditors, management, and other stakeholders in making informed decisions.

3.8 Chapter Summary

As the language of business, accounting is indispensable for both profit and nonprofit organizations. It involves recording, summarizing, and analyzing financial transactions, which helps organizations monitor their financial health, profitability, and sustainability. For-profit organizations utilize accounting to prepare financial statements, calculate profits and losses, assess cash flows, and ensure compliance with taxation and regulatory standards. Nonprofit organizations use accounting to maintain transparency, manage donor contributions, allocate funds to various projects, and demonstrate accountability to their stakeholders. Effective accounting practices enable organizations to manage their resources efficiently, assess performance, and fulfill their financial obligations, contributing to overall success and sustainability.

3.9 Case Study: Informed Investment Decision through Reliable Accounting Data

(Scenario 1)

Overview: Riaz Alkozai, an experienced investor, is considering investing in Star Light Consulting LLC, a medium-sized consulting startup. To make an informed investment decision, Riaz relies on the company's financial statements for 2021 and 2022, which provide valuable insights into its financial health and potential for growth.

The Situation: Star Light Consulting LLC operates in the competitive field of consulting development, offering innovative solutions in the investment sector. Riaz is impressed by the company's product and potential to disrupt the market. However, before committing his funds, Riaz wants to ensure the company's financial stability and growth prospects.

Reliable and Credible Accounting Data: Riaz examines Star Light Consulting LLC's financial statements for 2021 and 2022, including the balance sheet, income statement, and cash flow statement. These statements provide a comprehensive overview of the company's financial position, performance, and cash flow during the year.

Key Indicators:

1. **Revenue Growth**: Riaz noticed a significant increase in the company's revenue compared to the previous year. This suggests strong market demand for the company's products.
2. **Profitability**: The income statement reveals that Star Light Consulting LLC's net income has increased, indicating that the company is effectively managing its costs and generating profits.
3. **Cash Flow**: Riaz carefully reviews the cash flow statement to assess the company's ability to generate cash from its operating activities. Positive cash flow from operations indicates the company's ability to fund its operations without relying heavily on external financing.
4. **Debt Levels**: The balance sheet shows that Company Star Light Consulting LLC's debt levels are manageable and in line with industry norms. This indicates prudent financial management and reduces the risk of insolvency.

Informed Investment Decision: Based on the reliable and credible accounting data in Star Light Consulting LLC's financial statements, Riaz gains confidence in the company's financial health and growth potential. The positive indicators of revenue growth, profitability, healthy cash flow, and manageable debt levels align with John's investment criteria.

Investment Outcome: Riaz invests a substantial amount in Star Light Consulting LLC, recognizing that the company's financial strength and promising growth trajectory make it an attractive opportunity for long-term returns. Over the next few years, Star Light Consulting LLC will successfully expand its market presence and realize its growth projections, resulting in a profitable investment for Riaz.

This scenario exemplifies the critical role of reliable and credible accounting data in guiding investor decisions. By thoroughly analyzing a company's financial statements, investors can gain insights into its financial health, growth prospects, and overall risk profile, enabling them to make informed investment choices that align with their objectives.

Star Light Consulting LLC
Income Statement
as of December 31

	2021	2022
Revenue		
Consulting Services	$1,245,965.00	$1,854,875.00
Total Revenue	$1,245,965.00	$1,854,875.00
Less Expenses		
Advertising	$118,091.45	$123,996.02
Bank Charges	$8,957.71	$9,405.60
Insurance	$1,864.44	$1,957.66
Legal and Professional Fees	$16,305.86	$171,121.15
Office Expense	$28,348.48	$29,765.90
Vehicle Expense	$73,486.33	$106,948.60
Payroll -Wages & Salaries	$461,007.05	$695,955.00
Payroll Taxes	$35,267.04	$53,240.56
Rent	$158,100.00	$158,100.00
Telephone Expense	$39,010.32	$48,552.00
Utilities	$26,233.03	$35,628.00
Total Expenses	$966,671.71	$1,434,670.49
Net Profit/Loss	$279,293.29	$420,204.51
Less Corp Taxes	$61,444.52	$92,444.99
	$217,848.77	**$327,759.52**

Star Light Consulting LLC
Balance Sheets
as of December 31

	2021	2022
Current Assets		
Cash	$190,675.00	$236,500.62
Account Receivables	$497,870.00	$478,715.90
Short-Term Notes Receivables	$127,545.00	$385,435.00
Total Current Assets	$816,090.00	$1,100,651.52
Fixed Assets		
Office Furniture	$71,164.00	$71,164.00
Computers and Software	$32,992.00	$52,992.00
Vehicles	$120,098.00	$149,121.00
Total Fixed Assets	$224,254.00	$273,277.00
Total Assets	**$1,040,344.00**	**$1,373,928.52**
Current Liabilities		
Account Payable	$25,766.00	$28,765.00
Short Term Loans	$48,101.00	$63,567.00
Total Current Liabilities	$73,867.00	$92,332.00
Long Term Loans	$93,650.00	$62,545.00
Total Liabilities	$167,517.00	$154,877.00
Equity		
Paid In Capital	$275,000.00	$275,000.00
Returned Earnings	$306,111.23	$523,960.00
Net Profit/ Loss	$217,848.77	$327,759.52
	$798,960.00	$1,126,719.52
	$1,040,344.00	**$1,373,928.52**

(Scenario 2)

Budget Planning and Control for Royal Lodge

Introduction

Budget planning and control are the most important tools managers must use to guarantee a company's long-term sustainability. To run a successful business, managers must plan and have a practical set of internal controls to ensure compliance with management's policies and procedures.[33] We have various methods for managing the organization's budget, but the most used are variance analysis and forecasting. If Royal Lodge is facing a financial challenge based on its actual receipts, an action plan needs to be taken to resolve this misalignment.

Let's describe and provide a brief overview of Royal Lodge, determine the reasons for preparing and managing budgets, outline a high-level budget plan, propose some methods and techniques for managing the budget, and prepare an action plan to resolve the budget misalignment.

Description of the Company

Royal Lodge is a partnership company established in September 2013 by Orphelia Buttermilk and Okaine Newman. They have been friends since college, and both have undergraduate degrees in marketing.

The Royal Lodge was initially known as the Coach House Bed and Breakfast. It was built in 1939 and is believed to have been one of the few hotels that housed visitors searching for a mountain escape in the Black Mountain area of Buncombe County in Ashville, North Carolina, in the United States of America. The lodge is a "paradise away from home" and offers 30 individually furnished rooms, each with a mountain theme.[34]

With its 12 employees, the Royal Lodge provides a serene setting for its guests to enjoy the many splendors of the beautiful North Carolina mountains and natural walking and hiking trails.

---

[33] Koutoupis, A. G., & Malisiovas, T. (2023). The effects of the internal control system on the risk, profitability, and compliance of the US banking sector: A quantitative approach. *International Journal of Finance & Economics, 28*(2), 1638-1652.

[34] TripAdvisor, LLC (2023) Ashville Hotels. Retrieved from http://www.tripadvisor.com/hotels-g60742-Ashville_North_Carolina-Hotels.html.

Also, with the economy picking up and the Ashville government bringing more tourism attractions to the area, Royal Lodge plans to expand its rooms from 30 to 35. In addition, Royal Lodge projects a modest 30% increase in unit rental per year for the following years. This projection is based on the general average increase in tourism in the Ashville area, which saw the annual occupancy rate go up from $69.00 in 2009 to $112.00 in 2022, with revenue of $987,800 in the 2021 fiscal year.

The Royal Lodge wanted to oversee and produce proper budget planning and control to maintain its activity level and increase its success and profitability.

Reasons to Prepare and Manage a Budget of the Company

As explained above, many reasons exist to prepare and manage a budget, especially for small, growing businesses. First, preparing and managing a budget should be possible for management to maintain enough cash to pay creditors, to have sufficient raw materials to meet production requirements, and to have adequate finished goods to meet expected sales.

A second reason the Royal Lodge needs to prepare and manage a proper budget is to evaluate performance at each level of responsibility. The 2022 budget provides historical data on revenues, costs, and expenses, which will help formulate future budget goals for the company.

One positive financial outcome for Royal Lodge to perform proper effective budgeting is to facilitate the reconciliation of activities within the business in integrating production and sales promotion with expected sales.

Again, proper budgeting will result in greater management awareness of the company's overall operations and the impact of external factors on operations, such as economic trends. There are also some adverse financial outcomes that the Royal Lodge can face by producing poor budgeting. For example, the company can experience poor liquidity due to mismanagement, affectation of funds, and the risk of filing for bankruptcy if the business turns down.

High- Level Budget Plan for the Company

To meet sales requirements, Royal Lodge needs to establish a high-level budget that summarizes estimated costs to help achieve its financial goals. This high-level budget includes various rubrics such as direct materials purchases, advertising, taxes, and so on, which are very important for the company. The most appropriate budgeting phases for the company are:

- First, the preparation of operating and financial programs by integrating all departments' considerations into the final budget.
- Phase 2 is the budget approval. This includes budgetary priorities after adjusting the final budget.
- The third phase is executing the budget by the chief executive after making some final adjustments according to the budgetary needs.
- The final phase is evaluating the budget by the company's managers and other stakeholders. This phase is the most critical budgeting phase for the company since it shows a clear picture of its budget. Thus, managers and stakeholders (owners) can decide to correct all discrepancies.

To illustrate all the information given above, here is a sample of the Royal Lodge's sales budget.

ROYAL LODGE
Selling and Administration Expense Budget
For the Year Ending December 31, 2022

	Quarter				
	1	2	3	4	Year
Budget Sales in Units	2,720	2,730	2,725	2,730	10,905
Variable expenses					
Sales commissions (10$ per unit)	$27,200	27,300	27,250	27,300	109,050
Total variable expenses	$27,200	$27,300	$27,250	$27,300	$109,050
Fixed expenses					
Advertising	30,000	30,000	30,000	30,000	120,000
Sales salaries	23,000	23,000	23,000	23,000	92,000
Property taxes and insurance	1,000	1,000	1,000	1,000	4,000
Total fixed expenses	54,000	54,000	54,000	54,000	216,000
Total selling and administrative expenses	$81,200	$81,300	$81,250	$81,300	$325,050

Methods and Techniques for Managing the Budget

Numerous methods exist to manage and prepare the budget over time. One such technique is budget forecasting, which prevents expenditures from going too far by making realistic predictions of where to allocate resources. The forecast can be made monthly, quarterly, or yearly to avoid financial uncertainties.

Another important method for managing the budget over time is periodic variance analysis. In this method, we look at the deviations in the cost of raw materials, labor, and revenue from the budget estimation. Analyzing budget variances monthly can help take corrective action and ensure the budget is within its intended range.

Action Plan for Resolving the Budget Misalignment

If there is a misalignment due to financial challenges, action must be taken to resolve this discrepancy. The best way to resolve the budget and actual discrepancies will be using Zero-Based Budgeting (ZBB). Zero-based budgeting is a method of budget preparation that begins each period with a clean slate. Under this technique, managers must start from zero and justify budgets periodically.

Also, managers must analyze the activity's cost, identify alternative ways of achieving it, establish activity performance, and so on by describing activities in a" decision package." Thus, the manager can identify and eliminate inefficient activities and spending. Using zero-based budgeting will help in efficient resource allocations and resolve budget misalignment.

Conclusion

According to all the information above, proper budget planning and control can positively impact the management of a company such as Royal Lodge. Failure to prepare or present effective budgeting can have some consequences, like filing for bankruptcy. So, to prevent and ensure success, the Royal Lodge has to use effective budget management techniques to elaborate appropriate high-level budgets.

3.10 Quiz To Assess Knowledge of Chapter 3

1. What is the primary purpose of financial accounting?
    a) Internal decision-making
    b) External reporting to stakeholders
    c) Employee payroll management
    d) Strategic planning
2. Which accounting equation represents the fundamental relationship in accounting?
    a) Assets = Liabilities + Equity
    b) Revenue = Expenses
    c) Debits = Credits
    d) Profit = Revenue - Expenses
3. What is the importance of the accrual basis of accounting?
    a) Recognizes transactions only when cash is received or paid.
    b) Matches revenues and expenses when they are earned or incurred.
    c) Records transactions at the time they are contracted.
    d) Focuses on the cash flow statement.
4. Which financial statement provides a snapshot of a company's financial position at a specific point in time?
    a) Income statement.
    b) Cash flow statement.
    c) Balance sheet.
    d) Statement of retained earnings.
5. What type of account is "Accumulated Depreciation"?
    a) Revenue account
    b) Expense account
    c) Asset account
    d) Liability account

6. What accounting assumption assumes a business will continue operating indefinitely?
    a) Materiality assumption
    b) Going concern assumption.
    c) Consistency assumption
    d) Monetary unit assumption
7. Which financial statement reports a company's revenues and expenses over a specific period?
    a) Balance sheet
    b) Income statement
    c) Statement of cash flows
    d) Statement of retained earnings.
8. What is the formula for calculating the return on equity (ROE)?
    a) Net Income / Average Total Assets
    b) Net Income / Average Shareholders' Equity
    c) Total Revenue / Average Total Assets
    d) Total Revenue / Average Shareholders' Equity
9. Which of the following is an example of an intangible asset?
    a) Buildings
    b) Land
    c) Patents
    d) Inventory
10. What is the purpose of the statement of cash flows?
    a) To report a company's financial position at a specific time.
    b) To provide information about a company's liquidity and cash flow activities.
    c) To detail changes in equity over a specific period
    d) To report revenues and expenses over a specific period

3.11 Answers to the Quiz and Explanations of Correct Answers

1. Answer B

The primary purpose of financial accounting is to provide relevant, reliable, and timely financial information that facilitates decision-making, transparency, and accountability for a wide range of stakeholders in and outside the organization.

2. Answer A

The accounting equation must always be balanced, meaning that a business's total assets must equal the sum of its liabilities and equity. This reflects the basic accounting principle that every transaction has a dual effect, impacting both the left side (assets) and the right side (liabilities and equity) of the equation.

3. Answer B

The accrual basis of accounting is essential because it matches revenues and expenses with the periods in which they are earned or incurred rather than when the cash is received or paid. This accounting method provides a more accurate representation of a company's financial position.

While the accrual basis of accounting provides a more accurate representation of a company's financial activities, it requires careful tracking of receivables, payables, and other non-cash transactions. Cash transactions are recognized only when cash is exchanged.

4. Answer C

The balance sheet is a financial statement that provides a snapshot of a company's financial position at a specific time. Along with the income and cash flow statements, it is one of the three primary financial statements. The balance sheet is sometimes called a "statement of financial position" because it summarizes a company's assets, liabilities, and equity.

The balance sheet equation, as mentioned earlier, is Assets = Liabilities + Equity

5. Answer C

The account "Accumulated Depreciation" is classified as a contra-asset account. It records the total depreciation expense charged against a company's assets over time. The Accumulated Depreciation has a credit balance, which is the opposite of the usual debit balance for assets.

6. Answer B

The accounting assumption that assumes a business will continue operating indefinitely is called the "going concern assumption." This assumption is a fundamental principle in financial accounting and financial reporting.

The going concern assumption implies that when preparing financial statements, accountants assume that the entity will remain in operation for the foreseeable future, typically the next 12 months or more. This assumption is crucial for the proper application of accounting principles and the presentation of financial information.

7. Answer B

The income statement, also known as the profit and loss statement or statement of earnings, is a financial statement that reports a company's revenues and expenses over a specific period. Its primary purpose is to show the business's profitability during the reporting period. It summarizes how well the company generated revenue, controlled expenses, and ultimately earned a profit or incurred a loss.

8. Answer B

The Return on Equity (ROE) is a financial ratio that measures the profitability and efficiency with which a company uses its shareholders' equity to generate profit.

Return on Equity (ROE)=Net Income/Average Shareholders' Equity

ROE is a crucial metric for investors and analysts, providing insights into the company's ability to generate profits from shareholders' investments. However, it's important to consider industry benchmarks and compare ROE with other financial ratios to comprehensively analyze a company's financial performance. Industries may have different typical ranges for

ROE due to variations in business models, capital structures, and risk profiles.[35]

9. Answer C

Patents are indeed an example of an intangible asset. Intangible assets lack physical substance but hold economic value for a company. Patents expressly represent exclusive rights granted by a government to an inventor or assignee for a limited period, usually 20 years, to exclude others from making, using, or selling an invention.

Other examples of intangible assets include trademarks, copyrights, goodwill, trade secrets, and customer lists. Intangible assets are crucial for many businesses, especially those in technology, pharmaceuticals, and other industries where innovation and intellectual property play a significant role. Proper accounting and reporting of intangible assets, including patents, are essential for providing a comprehensive and accurate picture of a company's financial position.

10. Answer B

The primary purpose of the statement of cash flows is to provide information about a company's liquidity and cash flow activities during a specific period. Along with the income statement and the balance sheet, it is one of the three primary financial statements.

The statement of cash flows provides a comprehensive view of a company's cash inflows and outflows. Its primary purpose is to assess the company's ability to generate and manage cash, evaluate liquidity, and understand the impact of various cash flow activities on the business.

[35] Huang, Y. C., Han, L. X., & Xie, W. H. (2024, March). Application of Big Data Analysis in Identifying Problems in Financial Reporting of BYD Company. In Modern Economic Management Forum (Vol. 2, No. 1).

Chapter 4

Finance in Business Management

4.1 Introduction

In the dynamic and fast-paced world of business management, finance emerges as a driving force that shapes the financial landscape of organizations, both big and small. Chapter 4 of this comprehensive business management guide explores the crucial role of finance in steering businesses toward success, growth, and financial sustainability. As a discipline governing financial resource allocation, management, and utilization, finance is at the heart of strategic decision-making, investment planning, and risk assessment.

In this chapter, we delve into the multifaceted applications of finance in business management, uncovering its significance in optimizing profitability, managing working capital, and ensuring long-term financial stability. At its core, finance empowers managers to make informed choices that align with the organization's objectives, seeking opportunities for growth while mitigating potential risks.

We begin by understanding financial management principles and examining the essential concepts of the time value of money, risk and return, and the cost of capital. These foundational elements are the building blocks for evaluating investment opportunities, analyzing capital budgeting decisions, and determining the optimal capital structure.

As we delve deeper, we explore the role of finance in financial planning and forecasting. Managers gain valuable insights into resource allocation, revenue, and expense management through budgeting and financial projections, ensuring a sound financial roadmap for the organization's future.

Moreover, this chapter also touches upon the significance of financial analysis in business management. We unravel the techniques and tools employed to evaluate financial performance, analyze financial statements, and assess the organization's liquidity, profitability, and solvency.

Finance is pivotal in making critical investment decisions in pursuing growth and expansion. We navigate through investment analysis principles, understanding how organizations identify lucrative opportunities, diversify portfolios, and assess risk-reward trade-offs.

Furthermore, risk management is an integral part of finance in business management. From identifying and evaluating risks to implementing strategies for risk mitigation, managers rely on financial expertise to safeguard the organization's interests and ensure resilience in the face of uncertainties.

As we journey through Chapter 4, it becomes evident that finance is not merely a department within an organization but a strategic partner influencing decision-making at every level. From startups seeking funding to established enterprises optimizing their financial performance, finance principles remain a cornerstone in driving business success.

Join us in exploring Chapter 4 as we unravel the intricacies of finance in business management. This discipline equips managers with the financial acumen to navigate challenges, seize opportunities, and lead their organizations toward prosperity in an ever-evolving business landscape. From financial planning to investment analysis, from risk management to performance evaluation, the principles of finance guide managers on a path toward sustainable growth and financial excellence.

4.2 What is Finance?

Finance is the field of study that deals with managing an organization's money, investments, and financial resources. It involves making decisions about acquiring, allocating, and utilizing funds to achieve the organization's objectives. Finance encompasses various activities, including financial planning, budgeting, investment analysis, risk management, and capital allocation.

The role and importance of finance in both profit and nonprofit organizations are significant and include the following:

1. Capital Acquisition: Finance helps organizations determine the most appropriate funding sources, such as equity, debt, or retained earnings, to support their operations and growth. It involves decisions related to raising capital from investors or borrowing from financial institutions.
2. Investment Decisions: Finance is critical in evaluating investment opportunities and determining the best allocation of funds. Organizations

analyze potential projects, acquisitions, or expansions to assess their financial viability and potential returns.

3. Financial Planning and Budgeting: Finance is instrumental in creating financial plans and budgets that align with the organization's strategic objectives. It involves forecasting future financial needs, estimating revenues and expenses, and setting financial targets.
4. Risk Management: Finance helps organizations identify and manage financial risks, such as market fluctuations, interest rate changes, or credit risks. Effective risk management strategies are essential for both profitability and financial stability.
5. Working Capital Management: Finance oversees the management of short-term assets and liabilities to ensure smooth day-to-day operations. Proper working capital management is crucial to maintaining liquidity and meeting short-term financial obligations.
6. Financial Analysis: Finance utilizes various financial ratios, metrics, and tools to analyze the organization's financial performance and health. This analysis guides decision-making identifies areas for improvement and facilitates long-term planning.
7. Cost Control and Profitability: Finance aids in cost control initiatives to enhance profitability. It involves analyzing cost structures, identifying cost-saving opportunities, and optimizing resource allocation.
8. Financial Reporting and Compliance: Finance produces financial reports and statements that adhere to accounting standards and regulatory requirements. Accurate and timely financial reporting is essential for external stakeholders and internal management.
9. Asset Management: Finance oversees the management of the organization's assets, including investments, inventory, and fixed assets. Proper asset management ensures optimal utilization and maximization of returns.

4.3 The Role of Finance

The role of finance within a business or organization encompasses a range of critical functions that contribute to its overall success and sustainability.

Finance is crucial in organization management because it provides the framework for making strategic decisions, managing resources, and achieving financial objectives. It helps organizations allocate funds effectively, invest wisely, manage risks, and ensure long-term financial sustainability. Without sound financial management, organizations would struggle to meet their financial obligations, capitalize on growth opportunities, and maintain competitiveness in the market. Effective finance management is crucial in achieving profit and nonprofit organizations' success, growth, and profitability.

Here's an overview of the mentioned roles in finance:

1. **Investment:** Finance plays a pivotal role in making investment decisions that maximize the value of the organization's assets. This involves evaluating potential investment opportunities, such as projects, acquisitions, or new ventures, to determine their potential risks and returns. Financial analysts use tools such as Net Present Value (NPV), Interest Rate of Return (IRR), and payback period to assess and prioritize investments that align with the company's strategic goals and generate positive cash flows.
2. **Fraud, Internal Control, and Cash Management**: Finance establishes and maintains internal control systems that safeguard the company's assets and ensure accurate financial reporting. This includes implementing procedures to prevent fraud, detecting errors, and ensuring compliance with regulations. Additionally, finance manages cash flow by monitoring cash inflows and outflows, optimizing working capital, and maintaining appropriate levels of liquidity to meet operational needs and financial obligations.
3. **Cash Flows Analysis**: Finance professionals play a crucial role in preparing and analyzing the statement of cash flows. This statement provides insights into how cash is generated and used within the organization, categorizing cash flows into operating, investing, and financing activities. Effective cash flow management is essential for maintaining financial stability, funding growth initiatives, and meeting financial obligations.
4. **Financial Statement Analysis**: Finance experts analyze financial statements to assess a business's financial health and performance. They evaluate critical liquidity, solvency, profitability, and efficiency indicators through ratio, trend, and benchmarking analysis. This analysis helps stakeholders understand the company's financial strengths and weaknesses, make informed investment decisions, and identify areas for improvement.

4.4 Different Types of Finance in Organizations

Finance in organizations can be broadly categorized into several types or categories, each serving specific functions and contributing to the overall financial management and decision-making process. Here are some of the main categories of finance within an organization:

1. **Corporate Finance**: Corporate finance involves managing a company's financial resources to achieve its overall goals and maximize shareholder value. It includes activities such as capital budgeting (deciding on investments), capital structure management (mix of equity and debt), and dividend policy (how profits are distributed to shareholders). Corporate finance also involves financial analysis, risk management, and financial planning.
2. **Managerial Finance**: Managerial finance focuses on the financial decisions made within the organization's specific department or business unit. Managers use financial data and analysis to make decisions related to budgeting, cost control, resource allocation, and investment opportunities. This type of finance helps operational managers ensure the efficient use of resources.
3. **Investment Finance**: Investment finance evaluates various investment opportunities and makes informed decisions about allocating funds to different assets or projects. This category involves portfolio management, asset allocation, risk assessment, and analysis of financial markets to optimize returns while managing risks.
4. **Financial Risk Management**: Financial risk management involves identifying, assessing, and mitigating various financial risks an organization might face. This includes credit risk (risk of non-payment by borrowers), market risk (risk due to changes in market prices), operational risk (risk from internal processes), and liquidity risk (risk of insufficient funds to meet financial obligations).
5. **International Finance**: International finance deals with financial transactions and decision-making across international borders. It includes foreign exchange management, assessing and managing global investment opportunities, and navigating the complexities of regulatory environments and currency fluctuations.
6. **Public Finance**: Public finance deals with governments' and public entities' financial activities and decisions. It encompasses government revenue generation (taxation), public expenditure allocation, public debt management, and economic stabilization policies.
7. **Behavioral Finance**: Behavioral finance explores the psychological and emotional factors influencing individuals' and organizations' financial

decisions. This field examines how cognitive biases and emotions can lead to irrational behavior and impact financial outcomes.

8. **Personal Finance**: Personal finance focuses on managing individual or household finances, including budgeting, saving, investing, and retirement planning. While not directly tied to organizational finance, employees' financial well-being can indirectly impact their productivity and job satisfaction.
9. **FinTech and Innovation Finance**: With the rise of technology and innovation, finance has also evolved to include FinTech (Financial Technology) and innovation finance. This involves leveraging technology to develop new financial products, services, and platforms to streamline processes, enhance customer experiences, and provide novel solutions.

These finance categories work together to ensure an organization's financial resources are effectively managed, risks are identified and mitigated, investments are well-chosen, and financial goals are achieved.

4.5 Chapter Summary

The role of finance is multifaceted. It encompasses various responsibilities, from evaluating investment opportunities to ensuring internal controls, managing cash flow, and conducting thorough financial statement analysis. Finance professionals contribute to strategic decision-making by providing insights that drive growth, mitigate risks, and enhance the overall financial well-being of the organization.

Finance is also essential to organizational management, as it allocates and manages financial resources. For-profit organizations depend on finance to determine optimal capital structures, assess investment opportunities, manage working capital, and make strategic financial decisions. Nonprofit organizations use financial management to plan budgets, optimize fundraising efforts, and efficiently allocate resources to achieve their social or charitable objectives.

4.6 Case Study 1: Strategic Investment in the Blye Family LLC - A Sound Audit Report

Overview: The Blye Family LLC, a prominent financial firm, is considering a long-term investment in the hotel industry in Virginia, USA. The decision to invest is driven by a comprehensive audit report demonstrating sound financial management, strong cash flow, and no indication of fraud in the targeted hotel establishment.

The Situation: The Blye Family has identified a luxury hotel in Virginia as a potential investment opportunity. Before committing capital, The Blye Family LLC conducts due diligence to ensure the hotel's financial stability and growth potential.

The Audit Report: The Blye Family LLC commissions a reputable auditing firm to thoroughly audit the hotel's financial records for the past three years (2020, 2021, and 2022). The audit report reveals the following key findings:

1. **Clear Origin of Funds**: The audit confirms that the hotel's funds have been sourced legitimately and transparently. No irregularities or suspicious transactions raise concerns about the origin of capital.
2. **Strong Cash Flow Management**: The hotel's financial statements demonstrate consistent and healthy cash flow management. Revenue from room bookings, events, and other services is well-documented, and expenses are managed efficiently.
3. **Robust Cash Flow**: The hotel's cash flow projections indicate a steady and sustainable income stream, even during seasonal fluctuations. This suggests that the hotel can generate positive cash flow for operational expenses and debt service.
4. **Absence of Fraud Indicators**: The audit report confirms no signs of financial fraud, mismanagement, or unethical practices within the hotel's financial operations.

Strategic Investment Decision: Based on the audit report findings, The Blye Family LLC determines that the hotel represents a sound investment opportunity. The hotel's clear origin of funds, robust cash flow, strong cash management practices, and absence of fraud indicators align with the firm's investment criteria for long-term viability and growth potential.

Investment Strategy Implementation: The Blye Family LLC proceeds with a long-term investment in the hotel industry by acquiring a significant stake in the Virginia-based luxury hotel. The firm leverages its expertise in the hospitality sector to implement a strategic plan to enhance guest experiences, improve operational efficiency, and maximize returns.

Investment Outcome: Over the next several years, the hotel will experience steady growth in occupancy rates, revenue, and profitability. The successful execution of the investment strategy results in increased brand recognition, positive guest reviews, and enhanced market positioning for the hotel in the competitive Virginia hospitality industry.

This case study exemplifies the importance of a sound audit report in guiding financial decisions. By clearly understanding the hotel's financial health, cash flow, and management practices, the audit report empowers The Blye Family LLC to confidently invest in the hotel industry, ultimately leading to a successful and profitable long-term investment in Virginia, USA.

CASH FLOW	2020	2021	2022
CASH RECEIPTS/ Income from sales			
Cash Sales	$1,000,000	$1,020,000	$1,040,000
Total cash from sales	$1,000,000	$1,020,000	$1,040,000
Income from Financing			
Interest Income	$0	$888	$1,206
Total cash from Financing	$0	$888	$1,206
TOTAL CASH RECEIPTS	$1,000,000	$1,020,888	$1,041,206
CASH DISBURSEMENTS			
Inventory	$16,000	$16,320	$16,646
Operating Expenses	$110,216	$110,216	$110,216
Commissions/Returns & Allowances	$12,500	$12,750	$13,006
TOTAL CASH DISBURSEMENTS	$138,716	$139,286	$139,868
NET CASH FLOW	$861,284	$881,602	$901,338

Case Study 2: PSC 7-Eleven Financial Analysis

General Information of PSC 7-Eleven

Philippine Seven Corporation ("PSC") was registered with the Securities and Exchange Commission ("SEC") on November 23, 1982. It acquired from South Corporation (now Seven Eleven, Inc. or "SEI") of Dallas, Texas, the license to operate 7-Eleven stores in the Philippines on December 13, 1982. Operations commenced with the opening of its first store on February 29, 1984, at the corner of Kamias Road and EDSA Quezon City, Metro Manila. Considering the country's economic condition, the company grew slowly in its first few years.

The headquarters is in Mandaluyong City, Philippines.

PSC is currently operating in the United States of America 1,281 stores, 743 are franchise stores, and the remaining 538 are company-owned stores. Also, 7-Eleven operates in Taiwan, China, the Philippines, and Japan, with 8,200 stores. The 7-Eleven stores carry a wide range of beverages, food service items, fresh foods, hot foods, frozen foods, confectioneries, cookies and chips, personal care products, groceries, gas, and other daily needs and services for modern convenience for neighborhood residents, communities, students, and other urban shoppers.

Except for Earnings Per Share (EPS), the consolidated financial statement is presented in thousands of Philippine pesos, the parent company's location. As of December 31, 2014, the company had just, for example, revenue from merchandise sales of P 17,107,375, cost of merchandise sales of P 12,861,596, earnings per share of 1.91, and net cash flow of P 268,659; and in 2012 at the same date, the company had the revenue from merchandise sales P 11,713,760, cost of merchandises sales P 8,553,239, earnings per share 1.01 and net cash flow of P 20,885. In comparing these data from 2012 to 2014, it shows that revenue from merchandise sales increased by 46.0%, cost of merchandise sales increased by 50.4%, Earnings Per Share (EPS) increased by 89.1%, and the net cash flow increased by 7.8% [1]. These may be justified for numerous reasons.

The rationale for choosing PSC 7-Eleven will be discussed. The ratios and stock prices will be analyzed, the strategy to minimize the risk of investment will be explained, and some recommendations will be given.

The Rationale for Choosing PSC 7-Eleven

The choice of PSC 7-Eleven may be justified by its profitability, business size, and higher overseas expansion. PSC 7-Eleven is not only a national company but also an international business. It is well established anywhere it is located, environmentally responsible, respectful of government regulations, and considers competitors' actions before making any investment decision.[36]

Investor's Profile

Investors are generally interested in investing in a company with less risky and volatile stocks, especially in a company that makes more profit. Net margin (%) is one of the financial tools measuring the profitability of the company, and the determination of Profit Margin will help investors and managers to know if the price of goods is keeping pace with changes in the cost of inventory or if the company maintains an adequate margin between sales and expenses. So, the company must determine the Gross Profit Rate, a percentage, by dividing the Gross Profit by Net Sales and the Profit Margin, which measures the percentage of each dollar of sales resulting in Net income.

In analyzing the financial statement consolidated as shown below, it indicates that:

	2012	2013	2014
Gross Profit	3,146,534	3,472,020	4,245,779
Net Income	465,176	682,626	873,345
Profit Margin	3.51%	4.61%	4.92%
Earnings Per Share	1.01	1.49	1.91

From 2012 to 2014, Gross Profit increased by 34.9%, Net Income increased by 87.7%, and Earnings Per Share (EPS) increased by 89.1%. This means the average margin between the selling price and inventory cost is rising, the company has a favorable return on each peso of sales, and Earnings per Share are more profitable, which could attract investors who want to invest in the company.[37]

Also, the beta coefficient determination helps measure the volatility or the sensitivity of a company's share price or stock value relative to the general

[36] Financial Statement of 7-Eleven (2014). PSC Annual Report SEC Form. Retrieved from http://ww.7eleven.com.ph/investors_relation.php?title=Annual+Report

[37] Financial Statement of 7-Eleven (2014). PSC Annual Report SEC Form. Retrieved from http://www.7eleven.com.ph/investors_relation.php?title=Annual+Report

movement or the fluctuation in the current market price. It measures and ranks the systematic risks involved in the securities market, which is the relative volatility inherent in the general financial market and the organization system. If Beta equals 1, the average share or stock has a similar risk as the average market. If it is less than 1, the average market risk is below the average compared to the general market. If the Beta is greater than 1, it indicates that the average market risk and return is more than the average return of the entire market. PSC 7-Eleven Beta is 2.6, meaning it is more than one, and its risk is above the average return of the market at least 2.6 times more.

In short, PSC 7-Eleven, as a company, is a perfect fit to invest because the investor is young and has a long-term investment strategy.

Financial Ratio Analysis

Liquidity Ratio

Liquidity ratios indicate the company's ability to pay obligations expected to become due within the next year or operating cycle. As an investor, it is essential to know if the company meets its near-term debt to ensure it can pay its liabilities and maturing obligations and meet unexpected cash needs. So, determining Working Capital by subtracting Current Assets from Current Liabilities and Current Ratio by dividing Current Assets by Current Liabilities is crucial.

The current ratio of 7-Eleven indicates that the liquid assets ratios to the current liabilities are below the standard or minimum required of 1. A high current ratio could mean the company has a lot of money tied up in nonproductive assets, such as excess cash or marketable securities. Additionally, the company does not have favorable liquidity as it only has P0.80 in current assets for every peso invested in current liabilities. The company operated in 2014 with negative working capital, manifested by a current ratio of 0.80: 1 compared to 0.83: 1 in 2013. The proceeds from retail sales are invested in long-term assets and, at the same time, use the credit conditions granted by commercial suppliers. The company may be unable to pay its creditors in the short term and may be forced into bankruptcy.

Additionally, due to its lower current ratio, the company does not have favorable liquidity; for every dollar invested in current liabilities, it only has P0.80 in current assets.

		2014	2013
	Current Asse (A)	3,365,447,620	2,624,256,500
	Current Liability(B)	4,225,309,167	3,176,502,592
Working Capital	Difference (A)-(B)	(859,861,547)	(552,246,092)
Current Ratio	(A)/(B)	0.80:1	0.83:1

Profitability Ratio

Profitability is the net result of several policies and decisions, and the profitability ratios show the combined effects of liquidity, asset management, and debt on operating results.[38]

The Earnings per Share (EPS) for 7-Eleven from 2012 to 2014 were 1.01, 1.49, and 1.91 for the 3 years, respectively. The highest EPS was in 2014, while the lowest value was in 2012. Also, in analyzing the EPS trend for the 3 years, the tendency shows a net increase of 89.1% from 2012 to 2014, indicating that the business was profitable. The net profit margin and the return on asset (ROA) have increased to 40.2% and 37.7%, respectively, from 2012 to 2014.

Profitability	2012	2013	2014
EPS	1.01	1.49	1.91
ROA	8.75	11.27	12.05
Net Margin	3.51	4.61	4.92

Solvency Ratio

Solvency determines whether the company meets its long-term obligations by paying its interest when it comes due and repaying the debt balance owed at maturity.[39]

The Debt-to-Assets Ratio is a financial tool that measures a company's ability to survive for an extended period. It is computed by dividing total liabilities by assets; the minimum required rate is 1:1.

---

[38] Hussein, M. Q. S., Saeed, N. A., & Ahmad, G. S. (2023). Financial ratios analysis and companies' liquidity evaluation. *Journal of Global Economics and Business, 4*(14), 60-75.

[39] Malinowski, M. (2023). Solvency and Debt of Rural Communes vs. Their Residents' Standards of Living: A Polish Case Study. Agriculture, 13(12), 2222.

	2012	2013	2014
Total Assets	4,571,816,164	6,024,712,972	7,882,305,026
Total Liabilities	2,662,650,411	3,483,479,852	4,592,768,501
Debt to Asset Ratio	0.58	0.58	0.58

The company's debt-to-assets ratio remained at 0.58 from 2012 to 2014, which is required to achieve a medium value. This also means the company has tolerable solvency and can survive over a long period. Another critical element is the increase in its assets by 30.8% and its liabilities by 31.8% from 2012 to 2014, which indicates that the company has recently invested more money to boost its business.

Efficiency Ratio

This ratio shows how often the inventory turns in a year to generate revenue.[40] It is calculated by dividing the cost of goods sold by the average list. A higher ratio indicates better efficiency in the management of stock. The inventory turnover decreased not significantly from 2012 to 2014 and is still higher in 2014, with an average stock turnover of 13.31 times.

Moreover, the total asset turnover increased by 1.3% from 2012 to 2013 and failed again in the same range from 2013 to 2014, but it was still higher, with the average stocks turning 2.37 times in 2014, which is good.

	2012	2013	2014
Inventory Turnover	13.76	13.20	13.31
Total Asset Turnover	2.34	2.40	2.37

Leverage Ratio

The leverage ratio indicates how the company is financed. It shows how the company relies on foreign debts to fund its operations.

The operation leverage is calculated by dividing the net sales, fewer variables operating costs, and expenses by operating profit, and the financial leverage is computed by dividing operating profit by operating profit minus interest expenses. From 2012 to 2014, the financial leverage was at least in the same range of 1.0, but operating leverage decreased slightly from 2.28 to 2.27.

[40] Purnaningtyas, K. C. (2023). Analysis of Liquidity, Solvency, and Profitability Ratio to Assess the Financial Performance of PT Hamparan Estate Management in 2018-2020. *JOBS (Jurnal of Business Studies)*, *9*(1), 11-22.

	2012	2013	2014
Operating Leverage	2.28	2.09	2.27
Financial Leverage	1.01	1.01	1.00

Risk Level

There are no businesses without risk, especially in financial fields. PSC 7-Eleven risk management is integral to sound management practice and good corporate governance, improving decision-making and enhancing outcomes and accountability. PSC 7-Eleven recognizes that it has a responsibility to manage risks and supports a structured, systematic, and focused approach to managing them by approval of the risk management strategy.

The top risks in the retail industry to which PSC 7-Eleven belongs include economic slowdown, increase in competition, and brand reputation. Meanwhile, the main risks arising from the company's financial instruments are credit, liquidity, and interest rate risks.[41] To illustrate that, we have, for example:

Credit Risk

One party to a financial instrument will cause the other party an economic loss by failing to discharge an obligation or if the receivable balances are monitored continuously. To overcome these, the company's exposure to impairment arising from credit risk should be managed to a non-significant level.

Liquidity Risk

An entity will encounter difficulty meeting obligations associated with financial instruments, or the company seeks to manage its liquidity profile to finance its capital expenditures and service its maturing debts. In this case, the objective of the company's exposure to impairment-arising liquidity risk should be managed to a level that is not significant.

Interest Rate Risk (IRR)

Interest rate risk is the risk that a financial instrument's fair value or future cash flow will fluctuate because of changes in market interest rates or because the company is expanding to reduce the level of bank loans over time substantially[42].

[41] Shubbar, H. H. (2023). BANKING RISKS IN THE CONTEXT OF THE FINANCIAL CRISIS 2008. *World Bulletin of Management and Law,* 19, 136-142.
[42] Feng, X. (2024). A Study of Systemic Risk in the Banking Industry. *Highlights in Business, Economics and Management*, 24, 2416-2422.

The company's exposure to impairment arising from interest rate risk should be managed significantly.

Again, the best way to reduce or minimize the risks that are associated with investment is diversification. This involves portfolio management, which can be achieved by spreading over well-researched and profitable investments in the market that also promises good investment opportunities.

Recommendation

Investing in PSC 7-Eleven is an excellent opportunity for any investor or creditor interested in doing great business. PSC 7-Eleven has goodwill and positive prospects for getting money back. The Earnings per Share (EPS) for the last three years was very profitable, and the share percentage growth was 89.1% from 2012 to 2014. This indicates that 7-Eleven shares will most likely be accepted by a patient investor who wants to minimize risks and invest in shares that offer good returns.

Also, because the post's capital expenditures were primarily used to open new stores, expand store spaces, and set up logistic systems and related equipment, which were expected to improve its business, the latest investment will be welcomed in a better environment with established infrastructure. For all these reasons, investing in PSC 7-Eleven will be a vast window to raise businesses and make more profits.

PSC 7-Eleven is among the biggest companies in the United States of America. Its financial records and trends reflect that the company is growing year after year, and its future is very bright. Then again, even with tolerable liquidity, the company can survive an extended period because of its favorable solvency and return on each peso invested in its sales.

In 2014, the company was ranked number 10 on Entrepreneur Magazine's Top 500 list for 2015. Its primary competitors are EXXON Corporation, Royal Dutch SHELL, PLC, and Alimentation Couche-Tard Inc., which are also very big and multinational companies located in the United States of America.

In brief, we suggest investors buy its shares because the company is financially sound, environmentally responsible, runs its business guided by government laws, and considers the competitors' actions. All these show that one would get his money's worth if he invested in PSC 7-Eleven.

4.7 Quiz to Assess Knowledge of Chapter 4

1. What is the primary goal of financial management in a profit organization?
   a) Maximizing social impact.
   b) Maximizing shareholder wealth.
   c) Minimizing expenses.
   d) Achieving social responsibility.
2. What is a common source of funding for programs and initiatives in a nonprofit organization?
   a) Equity financing
   b) Grants and donations
   c) Issuing bonds
   d) Retained earnings.
3. What financial statement is crucial for assessing an organization's financial health and accountability?
   a) Income statement
   b) Statement of cash flows
   c) Balance sheet
   d) Statement of functional expenses
4. What term describes excess revenues over expenses in nonprofit finance?
   a) Profit
   b) Surplus
   c) Retained earnings.
   d) Shareholder wealth
5. Which financial ratio is particularly relevant for assessing a nonprofit organization's fundraising and administrative spending efficiency?
   a) Return on Assets (ROA)
   b) Fundraising efficiency ratio
   c) Debt-to-Equity ratio
   d) Operating margin

6. What is the primary objective of a for-profit organization's financial management regarding profitability?
    a) Break-even point
    b) Maximizing net income
    c) Minimizing donations
    d) Achieving program impact
7. What is the term for allocating costs to different programs and functions in nonprofit finance?
    a) Cost of goods sold
    b) Cost allocation
    c) Activity-based costing
    d) Programmatic expenses
8. What is the primary source of revenue for a for-profit organization?
    a) Grants and donations
    b) Program fees and services
    c) Investment income
    d) Sales of goods or services
9. How do nonprofit organizations measure success and impact financially?
    a) Profit margins
    b) Return on equity
    c) Social return on investment (SROI)
    d) Gross profit
10. What role does a finance committee typically play in the governance structure of nonprofit organizations?
    a) Setting marketing strategies
    b) Overseeing fundraising events
    c) Providing financial oversight and guidance.
    d) Implementing social programs.

4.8 Answer to the Quiz and Explanations of Correct Answers

1. Answer B

Maximizing shareholder wealth is often considered a for-profit organization's primary financial management goal. It means increasing the value of the shareholders' equity in the company, which is typically reflected in the stock price.

This objective aligns with the financial manager's responsibility to make decisions that enhance the company's long-term value, increasing shareholders' wealth. It implies a focus on profitability, effective use of resources, and strategic decision-making to ensure the company's sustained growth and competitiveness.

It's important to note that while maximizing shareholder wealth is a common goal, companies may also consider other objectives, such as maintaining financial stability, achieving growth, and ensuring corporate social responsibility. However, shareholder wealth maximization remains a fundamental guiding principle in financial management for for-profit organizations.

2. Answer B

Grants and donations are familiar funding sources for programs and initiatives in nonprofit organizations. Nonprofits often rely on external funding to support their mission and activities, and grants and donations are critical components of their revenue sources. Here's a brief explanation:

Grants: Nonprofit organizations may apply for and receive grants from government agencies, private foundations, corporations, and other grant-making entities. Grants are typically funding these organizations provide to support specific projects, programs, or initiatives that align with their mission and objectives. Nonprofits often compete for grants through a formal application process.

Donations: Donations come from individuals, businesses, and other organizations that contribute funds voluntarily to support the nonprofit's activities. Donations can be one-time gifts or recurring contributions and may be solicited through fundraising campaigns, events, or direct appeals. Donors are often motivated by a shared belief in the organization's mission or a desire to contribute to a cause they care about.

These funding sources are critical for nonprofits to carry out their work, serve their communities, and achieve their goals. Nonprofit organizations typically diversify their funding streams, incorporating a mix of grants, donations, and, in some cases, earned income (such as fees for services or products) to ensure financial sustainability. Proper financial management and transparency are essential in demonstrating accountability to donors and efficiently utilizing the funds to fulfill the organization's mission.

3. Answer C

The balance sheet is crucial for assessing financial health because it provides information about:

Liquidity: By analyzing current assets and liabilities, stakeholders can assess the organization's ability to meet its short-term obligations.

Solvency: Examining the proportion of assets financed by debt (liabilities) versus equity helps gauge the organization's long-term financial stability.

Financial Structure: The balance sheet reflects the composition of the organization's capital structure, showing the mix of debt and equity financing.

Net Worth: Shareholders' equity represents the organization's net worth, and changes over time indicate the impact of financial activities on the organization's overall value.

For accountability, the balance sheet, and other financial statements, such as the income statement and statement of cash flows, provide transparency into the organization's financial activities. This allows stakeholders, including investors, creditors, and donors, to make informed decisions and assess the organization's financial sustainability.

4. Answer B

In nonprofit finance, "surplus" describes excess revenues over expenses. A surplus is a positive financial outcome where the organization earned more revenue than incurred costs during a specific period.

Here's a breakdown of the terms:

Revenues: These are the funds a nonprofit organization receives, typically from various sources such as donations, grants, fundraising activities, program fees, or other income-generating activities.

Expenses: These are the costs and expenditures incurred by the nonprofit organization in carrying out its mission and programs. Expenses include salaries, rent, utilities, program, and administrative expenses.

Surplus: When the total revenues exceed the total expenses, the organization experiences a surplus. A surplus indicates that the nonprofit has generated more financial resources than it has spent during a specific reporting period.

A surplus is a positive financial outcome for a nonprofit organization as it contributes to its financial sustainability. This excess can be used for various purposes, such as:

Building Reserves: Surpluses can be set aside to create reserves or a financial cushion, providing the organization with a financial safety net for future uncertainties or emergencies.

Investing in Programs: Nonprofits may use surpluses to expand or improve their programs and services, increasing their impact on the community or cause they serve.

Strengthening Financial Position: Accumulating surpluses over time helps support the nonprofit's overall financial position and enhances its ability to weather economic challenges.

It's important to note that "surplus" is more commonly used in the nonprofit sector than "profit," which is associated with for-profit entities. Nonprofits focus on achieving financial sustainability and effectively using financial resources to fulfill their mission and serve their constituencies.

5. Answer B

The fundraising efficiency ratio is a financial ratio that is particularly relevant for assessing a nonprofit organization's efficiency in fundraising and administrative spending. This ratio provides insights into how effectively a nonprofit uses resources to generate funds for its programs and mission.

The fundraising efficiency ratio is calculated using the following formula:

Fundraising Efficiency Ratio = (Total Contributions – Fundraising Expenses) X100/ Total (Contributions)

In this formula:

Total Contributions: This includes all the funds the nonprofit receives from various sources, such as donations, grants, and fundraising events.

Fundraising Expenses: These are the costs associated with the organization's fundraising activities, including staff salaries, marketing materials, event costs, and other expenses related to raising funds.

The fundraising efficiency ratio measures what portion of total contributions remains after deducting the expenses related to fundraising. A higher fundraising efficiency ratio suggests that more contributions are available to support the organization's programs and mission, indicating greater efficiency in fundraising efforts.[43]

Nonprofit organizations aim to balance fundraising effectiveness and the costs associated with fundraising activities.

While a high fundraising efficiency ratio is generally positive, nonprofits need to consider other factors, such as the organization's overall financial health, the impact of fundraising efforts on program activities, and the long-term sustainability of fundraising strategies.

Donors and stakeholders often use the fundraising efficiency ratio to evaluate a nonprofit's financial transparency and resource stewardship.

6. Answer B

Maximizing net income is a for-profit organization's financial management objective regarding profitability. Net income, or net profit, is a vital indicator of a company's financial performance.

It represents the amount by which revenues exceed expenses during a specific period.

[43] Peng, S. (2024). Registration Level and Nonprofit Foundation Efficiency in China: The Moderating Role of Organizational Income.

The formula for calculating net income is:

Net Income=Total Revenues–Total Expenses

Here's why maximizing net income is a fundamental goal for for-profit organizations:

Shareholder Wealth Maximization: For-profit organizations are typically owned by shareholders, and maximizing net income increases shareholder wealth. Higher net income often leads to higher Earnings Per Share (EPS), positively impacting stock prices and shareholder returns.

Sustainability and Growth: A consistent and growing net income is crucial for a for-profit organization's long-term sustainability and growth. It provides the financial resources needed for investments in new projects, research and development, marketing, and other activities contributing to the company's expansion.

Creditworthiness: Maximizing net income enhances a company's creditworthiness. A profitable organization is better positioned to meet its financial obligations, attract investment, and negotiate favorable credit terms with creditors.

Market Competitiveness: Profitability is critical to assessing a company's market competitiveness. High net income allows a company to stay competitive by reinvesting in its operations, offering competitive pricing, and adapting to market changes.[44]

Return on Investment (ROI): Maximizing net income is essential for achieving a positive ROI. It reflects the effectiveness of the company's business activities in generating profits relative to the resources invested.

While maximizing net income is a primary objective, organizations need to balance profitability and other goals, such as maintaining financial stability, ensuring ethical business practices, and considering the interests of various stakeholders. Financial managers use different financial strategies and performance metrics to optimize net income while managing risks and uncertainties.

---

[44] Madura, J. (2015). *International financial management* (12th ed.). Stamford: CT: Cengage.

7. Answer B

In nonprofit finance, cost allocation refers to assigning or distributing costs to different organizational programs and functions. This method ensures that the various activities and services provided by the nonprofit bear a fair share of the organization's overall expenses.

8. Answer D

Sales of goods or services are typically the primary source of revenue for a for-profit organization. For-profit organizations intend to generate profit for their owners or shareholders, and one of the keyways they achieve this is by selling goods or providing services to customers.

9. Answer C

Social Return on Investment (SROI) is a financial metric used in nonprofit organizations to measure success and impact in financial terms. SROI goes beyond traditional financial measures by assessing the social, environmental, and economic value created by a nonprofit organization's activities.

SROI is part of a broader movement towards measuring and valuing social impact in a way that goes beyond traditional financial metrics. It helps nonprofits articulate their value proposition and demonstrate their meaningful contributions to society.

10. Answer C

Financial oversight and guidance are vital responsibilities that a finance committee typically plays in the governance structure of nonprofit organizations. The finance committee is a subcommittee of the board of directors and is specifically tasked with providing guidance and oversight on financial matters.

The finance committee is critical to the nonprofit organization's governance structure. It provides expertise and guidance to ensure sound financial management and accountability. Its work contributes to the organization's financial stability, sustainability, and ability to fulfill its mission effectively.

Chapter 5

Differences between Finance, Accounting, and Statistics

5.1 Introduction

In business and economics, three distinct disciplines play crucial roles: finance, accounting, and statistics. While these fields often overlap and interact, each serves a unique purpose in helping organizations make informed decisions and manage their resources effectively. This chapter will explore the key differences between finance, accounting, and statistics, supported by examples and a relevant case study.

While finance, accounting, and statistics serve unique functions, they aim to facilitate informed decision-making and optimize organizational performance [1]. As we delve into this chapter, we will uncover how these disciplines complement and interconnect, creating a powerful synergy that empowers managers to navigate challenges, seize opportunities, and drive success.

To begin with, we will unravel finance's fundamental nature, examining its focus on managing financial resources, evaluating investment opportunities, and ensuring optimal capital allocation. With an emphasis on financial planning and risk management, finance is a strategic partner that guides managers in making sound decisions for the organization's growth and stability.

Next, we delve into accounting, which revolves around the systematic recording, reporting, and analysis of financial transactions. As a foundation for financial information, accounting offers a clear view of an organization's financial health, enabling managers to assess performance, control costs, and ensure compliance with regulatory standards.[45]

On the other hand, statistics emerges as the data analysis science, allowing organizations to draw meaningful insights and make evidence-based decisions. We explore the role of statistics in processing data, identifying trends, and making predictions, making it an essential tool in finance and accounting.

---

[45] Kwok, S., Omran, M., & Yu, P. (Eds.). (2024). *Harnessing Technology for Knowledge Transfer in Accountancy, Auditing, and Finance*. IGI Global.

We will uncover their unique methodologies and techniques as we compare and contrast these disciplines. While statistics utilizes data sampling and inferential methods, accounting relies on double-entry bookkeeping and financial statement analysis, and finance applies financial modeling and investment valuation techniques.

Join us in exploring Chapter 5, where we unravel the intricate differences and similarities between finance, accounting, and statistics. As we navigate the dynamic landscape of business management, we will discover how leveraging the strengths of these disciplines empowers managers to make informed choices, optimize organizational performance, and steer their organizations toward prosperity in an ever-evolving and competitive global marketplace. From financial analysis to data-driven decision-making, risk assessment to strategic planning, and integrating finance, accounting, and statistics catalyzes sustainable growth in the organization.

5.2 Section 1: Finance

Finance studies how organizations manage their money and resources to achieve financial goals. It involves financial planning, investment decisions, capital management, and risk analysis to optimize the organization's financial resources. Finance also involves assessing financial risks, making investment decisions, and determining optimal capital structures. It is forward-looking and focuses on maximizing value and profitability. Critical financial concepts include the time value of money, risk, return, and financial markets.

Example: Calculating a project's Net Present Value (NPV) to assess its profitability over time.

5.3 Section 2: Accounting

Accounting is the systematic recording, analyzing, and reporting of financial transactions. Accounting focuses on recording, summarizing, and interpreting financial transactions to produce financial statements and reports. Accounting provides a historical view of an organization's financial performance and helps stakeholders understand its financial health.[46]

Accounting is governed by various principles and standards, such as Generally Accepted Accounting Principles (GAAP) or International Financial Reporting

[46] Nasim, K. T. (2024). Accounting Practices of NGO: A study on MAX Foundation.

Standards (IFRS). Critical financial statements include the balance sheet, income, and cash flow statements.

Example: Preparing an income statement to show a company's revenues, expenses, and profits.

5.4 Section 3: Statistics

Statistics involves collecting, analyzing, interpreting, and presenting data to gain insights and make informed decisions. Statistics involves collecting, analyzing, and interpreting financial data to draw meaningful insights and support decision-making. It provides tools for summarizing and understanding data variability, correlations, and trends.[47] In finance and accounting, statistics are often used for risk assessment, forecasting, and performance analysis.

Example: Analyzing historical stock price data to identify trends and patterns in market behavior.

5.5 Chapter Summary

While finance, accounting, and statistics share common ground in business decision-making, each field offers distinct perspectives and tools. Finance focuses on optimizing financial resources, accounting records historical financial data, and statistics extracts meaningful insights from data. The same is true of the economy, which refers to the production, distribution, and consumption system of goods and services within a region or country. The economy also encompasses all activities and interactions involved in creating and exchanging wealth, including the behavior of businesses, consumers, and governments. Integrating these disciplines enhances an organization's ability to make informed and successful strategic choices.

[47] JUBI, R. (2024). Business Analytics-Unleashing Data-Driven Decision Making. NEHAS PUBLICATIONS.

5.6 Case Study: Strategic Investment Decision

Imagine a manufacturing company, XYZ Corp., considering a significant investment in new technology to improve its production process. Let's explore how each discipline contributes to the decision-making process:

Finance: The finance department may assess the technology's potential Return On Investment (ROI). They calculate the NPV, considering the initial investment, expected cash flows, and discount rate. If the NPV is positive, it suggests that the investment is financially viable.

Accounting: The accounting department could examine the project's financial impact by estimating the cost of the technology, including depreciation and maintenance expenses. They prepare a projected income statement to show how the investment might affect profits over the next few years.

Statistics: The team may analyze historical data on production efficiency, costs, and revenues to build a forecasting model. They use regression analysis to determine the correlation between technology adoption and increased productivity, helping estimate future performance.

In this case study, finance evaluates the financial feasibility, accounting assesses the impact on financial statements, and statistics provides insights into potential outcomes.

5.7 Quiz to Assess Knowledge of Chapter 5

1. What is the primary focus of statistics?
    a) Recording financial transactions
    b) Analyzing and interpreting data.
    c) Managing organizational funds.
    d) Preparing financial statements.
2. Which discipline involves systematically recording, reporting, and analysis of financial transactions?
    a) Statistics
    b) Finance
    c) Accounting
    d) Economics
3. What is the primary goal of finance?
    a) Analyzing patterns in data.
    b) Maximizing shareholder wealth
    c) Preparing budgets and forecasts.
    d) Maintaining accurate financial records.
4. Which field focuses on managing funds within an organization, including investment decisions?
    a) Statistics
    b) Accounting
    c) Economics
    d) Finance
5. What role does statistics play in business decision-making?
    a) Analyzing financial transactions.
    b) Providing insights into market trends.
    c) Preparing income statements.
    d) Managing investment portfolios
6. In accounting, what is the primary purpose of financial statements?
    a) Analyzing economic trends.
    b) Providing information for decision-making.
    c) Maximizing shareholder wealth.
    d) Calculating statistical measures.
7. What discipline uses mathematical models to analyze and forecast financial markets?
    a) Statistics
    b) Accounting
    c) Economics

d) Finance

8. Which field is concerned with collecting, analyzing, and interpreting numerical data for various purposes?
   a) Accounting
   b) Finance
   c) Statistics
   d) Economics
9. What is the primary purpose of accounting principles and standards?
   a) Maximizing profits.
   b) Ensuring data accuracy.
   c) Facilitating economic analysis.
   d) Promoting ethical financial reporting.
10. Which discipline is closely tied to the study of economic systems, including the allocation of resources and decision-making?
   a) Statistics
   b) Accounting
   c) Economics
   d) Finance

5.8 Answer to the Quiz and Explanations of Correct Answers

1. Answer B

Statistics is a broad discipline that involves collecting, organizing, analyzing, interpreting, presenting, and drawing conclusions from data. While finance and accounting also include working with data, their primary focus is on the financial aspects of organizations. Finance manages money, investments, and financial markets, while accounting focuses on recording, summarizing, and analyzing financial transactions.

2. Answer C

Accounting is uniquely tailored to address the financial aspects of business operations, compliance with standards, and providing information for decision-makers within and outside an organization, distinguishing it from statistics and finance.

3. Answer B

The goal of maximizing shareholder wealth in finance reflects a specific orientation toward creating value for the business owners. This objective is distinct from the broader goals of statistics, which is focused on data analysis and interpretation, and accounting, which is centered around recording, reporting, and analyzing financial transactions. Each field serves different purposes within the broader context of business and decision-making.

4. Answer D

Finance encompasses various activities related to managing money and financial resources. Investment decisions are crucial in evaluating and selecting investment opportunities that align with the organization's financial goals.

5. Answer B

Instead of accounting and finance roles in business, statistics is a powerful tool in business decision-making, providing insights into market trends through data analysis. By leveraging statistical methods, companies can make informed decisions, identify opportunities, mitigate risks, and stay competitive in dynamic market environments.

6. Answer B

Accounting's primary purpose is to provide information for decision-making, and presenting sound financial statements is a crucial mechanism for achieving this goal. Financial statements are valuable for stakeholders to assess a business's financial health, performance, and prospects, ultimately guiding their decision-making processes.

7. Answer D

Mathematical models in finance enhance analytical capabilities, facilitate risk management, support decision-making, and provide a systematic framework for understanding and navigating the complexities of financial markets.

8. Answer C

Statistics is a branch of mathematics that deals with data collection, analysis, interpretation, presentation, and organization. It provides methods for making inferences and drawing conclusions from data and is used in various fields for different purposes.

9. Answer D

Promoting ethical financial reporting is indeed one of the primary purposes of accounting principles and standards. Ethical financial reporting ensures that financial information is accurate, transparent, and presented in a way that fairly represents an entity's financial position and performance. Accounting principles and standards are designed to establish a common framework for financial reporting, promoting consistency and comparability among financial statements.

10. Answer C

Economics is the social science that examines how societies allocate scarce resources to meet unlimited wants and needs. It involves studying economic systems, societies' structures, and processes to organize and coordinate the production, distribution, and consumption of goods and services.

Chapter 6

Similarities between Statistics, Accounting, and Finance

6.1 Introduction

Statistics, accounting, and finance are all managerial tools that effective managers need to know. Statistics, accounting, and finance are interconnected fields that share similarities due to their reliance on data analysis, numerical calculations, and decision-making.[48]

While finance, accounting, and statistics are distinct disciplines with unique roles, they also share several similarities that contribute to their interconnectedness and collaborative nature within a business. This chapter will delve into the commonalities between these fields, supported by examples and a relevant case study. Here are some examples of similarities between these disciplines:

6.2 Section 1: Data Analysis

All three disciplines involve data analysis to varying degrees. Statistics focuses on collecting, analyzing, and interpreting data to draw meaningful conclusions. Data analysis is crucial in accounting for recording financial transactions, preparing financial statements, and conducting audits. Finance relies on data analysis to assess investment opportunities, evaluate risks, and make informed financial decisions. The three disciplines heavily rely on data analysis to inform decision-making and provide insights. They utilize quantitative methods to process, interpret, and draw conclusions from data.

Example: In finance, data analysis is used to assess market trends and evaluate investment opportunities. In accounting, data analysis helps identify patterns of expenses and revenues. Data analysis is used in statistics to develop forecasting models and draw inferences from sample data.

---

[48] Cao, S. S., Jiang, W., Lei, L., & Zhou, Q. (2024). Applied AI for finance and accounting: Alternative data and opportunities. *Pacific-Basin Finance Journal*, 102307.

6.3 Section 2: Decision Making

Finance, accounting, and statistics provide valuable information that aids in making informed decisions. They help organizations allocate resources efficiently and effectively. Statistics, accounting, and finance contribute to informed decision-making. In statistics, data-driven decisions are made based on the analysis of empirical evidence. Accounting provides financial information that guides internal and external stakeholders in resource allocation, performance assessment, and investment decisions. Finance professionals make investment and funding decisions by analyzing financial data and considering factors like risk and return.

Example: In finance, decision-makers use financial ratios to evaluate a company's financial health and make investment decisions. In accounting, managers rely on financial statements to assess the performance of different departments. In statistics, decision-makers use regression analysis to determine the factors influencing a particular outcome.

6.4 Section 3: Risk Assessment

All three disciplines involve assessing and managing risk. In statistics, risk assessment is used to quantify uncertainty and variability in data analysis.

In finance, risk assessment is fundamental for evaluating investment opportunities, managing portfolios, and determining appropriate levels of risk exposure. Accounting also plays a role in risk assessment by providing information about a company's financial stability and potential vulnerabilities.[49] The three fields play a role in assessing and managing financial decisions and business operations risks.

Example: Risk assessment involves evaluating the potential risks and rewards of different investment options in finance. In accounting, risk assessment includes identifying potential financial misstatements or irregularities. In statistics, risk assessment helps determine the probability of various outcomes based on historical data.

[49] Țîrcovnicu, G. I., & Hațegan, C. D. (2023). Integration of Artificial Intelligence in the Risk Management Process: An Analysis of Opportunities and Challenges. *Journal of Financial Studies*, *8*(15), 198-214.

6.5 Section 4: Numerical Accuracy

All three fields emphasize the importance of numerical accuracy. In statistics, precise calculations are essential for accurate statistical analysis and interpretation. Accounting requires meticulous attention to detail to ensure accurate financial reporting and compliance with accounting standards. Finance professionals make critical decisions based on objective financial metrics, returns, and risk calculations.

Numerical accuracy is crucial in all three disciplines-statistics, accounting, and finance-to ensure reliable and precise results.

Example: Suppose a financial analyst calculates a company's Weighted Average Cost of Capital (WACC). They need accurate input data, including the cost of debt and equity, to determine the appropriate weights. Errors in these calculations could lead to inaccurate assessments of a company's investment opportunities.

6.6 Section 5: Regulatory Compliance

Statistics, accounting, and finance operate within regulatory frameworks. Statistics research must adhere to ethical guidelines and standards. Accounting follows Generally Accepted Accounting Principles (GAAP) or International Financial Reporting Standards (IFRS) to ensure consistent and transparent financial reporting. Finance professionals comply with financial regulations and legal requirements to provide ethical and legal financial practices.

Regulatory compliance is essential to maintain transparency, accountability, and adherence to industry standards.

Example: In accounting, a company must comply with Generally Accepted Accounting Principles (GAAP) or International Financial Reporting Standards (IFRS). Failure to accurately report financial data according to these standards could lead to legal and financial repercussions.

6.7 Section 6: Interdisciplinary Nature

These disciplines often overlap and interact. Financial data analyzed in statistics can contribute to financial analysis and decision-making in accounting and finance. Finance professionals use accounting data to analyze trends and forecast financial performance. Similarly, statistical methods are applied in finance and accounting for data analysis, risk assessment, and performance evaluation.

Interdisciplinary collaboration is joint among statistics, accounting, and finance to address complex business challenges.

Example: Consider a company's decision to expand into a new market. Finance assesses the financial feasibility and potential risks, accounting analyzes the costs and revenues associated with the expansion, and statistics models consumer behavior and market trends to provide insights into likely demand and revenue projections.

6.8 Chapter Summary

Despite their distinct focuses, finance, accounting, and statistics converge in their use of data, decision support, and risk assessment. Their similarities underscore the importance of interdisciplinary collaboration for well-informed business decisions. By leveraging the strengths of each field, organizations can achieve a holistic understanding of their financial landscape and optimize their operations for long-term success. The similarities between statistics, accounting, and finance highlight their interconnectedness and the shared importance of accurate data analysis, informed decision-making, and ethical practices in the business and financial world.

6.9 Case Study: Company X - Uniting Statistics, Accounting, and Finance

Overview: Company X is a global manufacturing corporation that produces consumer electronics. The company has a complex supply chain, operates in multiple countries, and faces dynamic market conditions. Company X aims to optimize its operations, enhance profitability, and mitigate risks while complying with regulatory standards. Also, X is seeking to allocate its budget for the upcoming fiscal year. Let's explore how each discipline contributes to this process:

Data Analysis: In pursuit of data-driven insights, Company X collaborates across its statistics, accounting, and finance departments. These teams analyze vast amounts of data to identify trends, patterns, and opportunities.

Example: The statistics team uses time series analysis to examine historical sales data, enabling them to uncover seasonal fluctuations and anticipate demand spikes. Accounting analyzes cost structures to identify areas for cost reduction, while finance evaluates data on market trends to determine potential new product lines.

Decision Making: Company X's decision-making process involves input from statistics, accounting, and finance. They work together to make informed strategic choices.

Example: The statistics team models potential market scenarios to estimate demand when launching a new product. Accounting assesses production costs and potential revenues, and finance evaluates the investment's financial viability, considering factors such as payback period and net present value.

Risk Assessment: Managing risks is a collaborative effort involving statistics, accounting, and finance to ensure the company's stability and sustainability.

Example: The finance team evaluates currency exchange rate risks, considering the impact of fluctuations on revenue and expenses. The statistics team employs regression analysis to identify variables influencing supply chain disruptions, aiding in proactive risk mitigation. Accounting assesses credit risks when dealing with international distributors.

Numerical Accuracy: Numerical accuracy is paramount across statistics, accounting, and finance to maintain reliable data-driven decision-making.

Example: Finance accurately calculates Return On Investment (ROI) to guide resource allocation. Accounting ensures the precise recording of financial transactions, such as inventory adjustments. Statistics maintains accurate data sets for predictive modeling, avoiding misleading insights.

Regulatory Compliance: Company X must adhere to its operations and financial reporting standards.

Example: Accounting ensures financial statements comply with International Financial Reporting Standards (IFRS) for accurate external reporting. Finance maintains compliance with tax regulations when expanding to new markets. Statistics ensures data privacy and compliance with data protection regulations.

Interdisciplinary Nature: The interdisciplinary collaboration between statistics, accounting, and finance enriches Company X's decision-making process.

Example: In a strategic pricing decision, finance evaluates profitability, accounting analyzes cost structures, and statistics models price elasticity to determine optimal pricing strategies.

Company X's success exemplifies the symbiotic relationship between statistics, accounting, and finance. By combining data analysis, decision-making, risk assessment, numerical accuracy, regulatory compliance, and interdisciplinary collaboration, Company X navigates challenges and seizes opportunities in the dynamic global business landscape. The integration of these disciplines strengthens the company's ability to make informed decisions, optimize performance, and sustain long-term growth.

6.10 Quiz to Assess Knowledge of Chapter 6

1. What is a common thread among statistics, accounting, and finance?
    a) Use of financial ratios
    b) Focus on analyzing market trends.
    c) Involvement in business decision-making
    d) Preparation of financial statements
2. Which area relies on numerical data to support decision-making processes?
    a) Statistics
    b) Finance
    c) Accounting
    d) All of the above
3. What is a shared goal of statistics, accounting, and finance in business contexts?
    a) Maximizing shareholder wealth.
    b) Minimizing expenses
    c) Facilitating informed decision-making.
    d) Conducting economic analyses.
4. In which discipline are quantitative skills essential for analyzing financial data?
    a) Statistics
    b) Finance
    c) Accounting
    d) Marketing
5. What do statistics, accounting, and finance contribute to in organizational settings?
    a) Strategic planning
    b) Legal compliance
    c) Human resource management
    d) Scientific research

6. What is a crucial information dissemination similarity between accounting and finance?
    a) Both produce financial statements.
    b) Both focus on statistical analysis
    c) Both involve economic forecasting.
    d) Both prioritize market research.
7. Which discipline is integral to assessing and managing risk in business operations?
    a) Statistics
    b) Accounting
    c) Finance
    d) Operations management
8. What is a common emphasis in using data in statistics, accounting, and finance?
    a) Analyzing consumer behavior.
    b) Understanding economic policies.
    c) Ensuring data accuracy and reliability.
    d) Conducting market research.
9. What is a shared focus when considering the time value of money in finance and accounting?
    a) Discounted cash flows
    b) Inflation rates
    c) Exchange rates
    d) Inventory turnover
10. What is a key role that statistics, accounting, and finance play in supporting organizational goals?
    a) Managing human resources.
    b) Enhancing social responsibility.
    c) Facilitating informed decision-making.
    d) Conducting scientific experiments.

6.11 Answer to the Quiz and Explanations of Correct Answers

1. Answer C

Involvement in business decision-making is common among statistics, accounting, and finance. In summary, statistics, accounting, and finance each contribute unique perspectives and tools to the decision-making process in business. Statistics provides the analytical foundation, accounting offers financial information for assessment, and finance guides strategic decisions related to investments, risk management, and capital structure. Together, these disciplines support a comprehensive approach to informed and effective decision-making within the business context.

2. Answer D

Statistics, finance, and accounting are all disciplines that heavily rely on numerical data to support decision-making processes in various fields. Here's how each of these areas uses numerical data. Using numerical data enhances precision, objectivity, and the ability to make data-driven decisions in all three areas. Whether analyzing trends in statistical data, assessing a company's financial health through accounting, or making investment decisions in finance, relying on numerical data is a common theme supporting rigorous analysis and informed decision-making.

3. Answer C

These disciplines provide information and insights that enable individuals and organizations to make well-informed decisions. The shared goal of statistics, accounting, and finance in a business context is to empower decision-makers with the information and tools needed to make informed choices. Whether it's analyzing data to identify trends, assessing financial performance, or evaluating investment opportunities, these disciplines contribute valuable insights that enhance the decision-making process within organizations.

4. Answer B

Quantitative skills are fundamental in finance because they enable professionals to analyze complex financial data, model financial scenarios, manage risks, and make informed investment decisions. The field of finance has become increasingly quantitative, using advanced mathematical models, statistical techniques, and data analytics to navigate the complexities of the financial markets.

5. Answer A

Statistics, accounting, and finance support strategic planning in organizational settings. Their contributions help organizations make informed decisions, allocate resources effectively, assess performance, and manage risks, which are crucial components of the strategic planning process.

6. Answer A

The production of financial statements is a crucial area where accounting and finance intersect. Accounting is primarily responsible for recording and summarizing financial transactions to generate these statements, while finance utilizes them as essential tools for analysis, valuation, and decision-making. The collaboration between accounting and finance ensures accurate and relevant financial information is disseminated to stakeholders for informed decision-making.

7. Answer C

Finance is integral to assessing, quantifying, and managing various types of risks in business operations. By understanding and mitigating risks, finance contributes to an organization's overall financial health and stability, supporting sustainable growth and resilience in a dynamic business environment.

8. Answer C

The emphasis on data accuracy and reliability is a shared principle in statistics, accounting, and finance. Data integrity is foundational to the credibility and usefulness of these disciplines' analyses, financial reporting, and decision-making processes. Establishing and maintaining high standards for data quality is crucial for the success and effectiveness of professionals in these fields.

9. Answer A

The consideration of discounted cash flows and the time value of money is a shared focus between finance and accounting. This concept is fundamental to various financial analyses, investment decisions, and accounting measurements, illustrating the interconnectedness of these disciplines in the business and financial landscape.

10. Answer C

Statistics, accounting, and finance are integral in facilitating informed decision-making within organizations. By providing reliable information, conducting data analyses, and assessing financial implications, these disciplines empower decision-makers to make choices aligned with organizational goals and contribute to overall success.

Chapter 7

Challenges between Statistics, Accounting, and Finance

7.1 Introduction

In the intricate web of business operations, statistics, accounting, and finance intersect, presenting opportunities and challenges for organizations. This chapter will explore some challenges when integrating these disciplines and discuss their impact on organizational success. We will also explore how the collaboration between finance, accounting, and statistics enhances data-driven decision-making, fosters effective resource allocation, and instills financial transparency and accountability. Each challenge is supported by examples in different sections, followed by a relevant case study illustrating the complexities involved.

7.2 Section 1: Data Consistency and Integration

Managers may face challenges integrating data from different sources, especially when dealing with vast and diverse datasets. Ensuring data accuracy and reliability is essential for making sound decisions.[50]

Challenge: Ensuring that data used by statistics, accounting, and finance teams are consistent and integrated to provide accurate insights.

Example: Discrepancies between financial data in the accounting department and sales data used by the statistics team can lead to inaccurate forecasts and financial misstatements.

7.3 Section 2: Interpretation Differences

Interpreting statistical results, financial statements, and complex financial data can be challenging. Managers need to communicate findings effectively to stakeholders with varying levels of financial literacy.

[50] Callahan, C. M. (2023). Evaluation for decision-making: The practitioner's guide to program evaluation. In *Systems and models for developing programs for the gifted and talented* (pp. 119-142). Routledge.

Challenge: Differences in interpreting data among statistics, accounting, and finance professionals can lead to conflicting analyses and decisions.

Example: A statistical analysis indicates a positive correlation between advertising spending and sales, while the finance team attributes an increase in sales to a recent cost-cutting measure instead.

7.4 Section 3: Regulatory Changes

Managers must handle data, financial reporting, and investment decisions with integrity and ethics. Ensuring transparency and compliance with relevant regulations is crucial.

Challenge: Adapting to regulatory frameworks and accounting standards impacting financial reporting and data analysis.

Example: Changes in tax regulations can affect financial projections and investment decisions, requiring finance and statistics teams to revise their models and forecasts.

7.5 Section 4: Risk Assessment Disparities

To effectively leverage these disciplines, managers must stay current with technological advancements in data analysis, accounting software, and financial management tools. Managers also often face balancing short-term financial performance with long-term strategic objectives. Effective financial planning and resource allocation are required to achieve this balance.

Challenge: There is variability in how statistics, accounting, and finance assess and manage risks, leading to inconsistent risk profiles.

Example: The statistics team identifies a high likelihood of supply chain disruptions, while the finance team considers the financial impact of such disruptions differently, affecting risk mitigation strategies.

7.6 Section 5: Communication Barriers

Interpreting statistical results, financial statements, and complex financial data can be challenging. Managers need to communicate findings effectively to stakeholders with varying levels of financial literacy.

Challenge: Overcoming communication barriers between statistics, accounting, and finance teams to facilitate effective collaboration.

Example: Misunderstandings between accounting and finance teams about terminology used in financial reports can hinder discussions about investment opportunities.

7.7 Chapter Summary

While integrating statistics, accounting, and finance offers significant benefits, it also presents unique challenges that organizations must navigate. By acknowledging and addressing these challenges, organizations can foster effective collaboration, enhance data accuracy, and make more informed decisions that drive sustainable success.

Statistics, accounting, and finance are indispensable for organizational success. While statistics, accounting, and finance aim to support data-driven decision-making and organizational management, they have distinct focuses, methodologies, and challenges. Addressing these challenges and integrating the strengths of each discipline can lead to more comprehensive and effective managerial decision-making and overall organizational success.

7.8 Case Study: Complex Investment Decision

Imagine a real estate development company, Property Ventures Inc., evaluating a large-scale investment project involving constructing residential complexes. Let's explore how the challenges play out:

Data Consistency and Integration: The accounting team records construction costs differently from how the statistics team categorizes them, leading to discrepancies in cost analysis.

Interpretation Differences: The statistics team's analysis of housing demand conflicts with the finance team's interpretation of market trends, resulting in disagreements over projected profits.

Regulatory Changes: A sudden change in zoning regulations impacts the project's feasibility, prompting the finance and statistics teams to recalibrate financial models.

Risk Assessment Disparities: The statistics team identifies potential climate-related risks, while the finance team focuses on financial risks, leading to a lack of alignment in risk mitigation strategies.

Communication Barriers: Complex financial terminology in project reports can confuse the accounting and finance teams during discussions on funding options.

In this case study, Property Ventures Inc. faces challenges in coordinating statistics, accounting, and finance efforts, illustrating the importance of addressing these challenges for successful decision-making.

7.9. Quiz to Assess Knowledge of Chapter 7

1. What challenge is expected of statistics, accounting, and finance when dealing with data?
    a) Data security
    b) Data accuracy and reliability
    c) Data visualization
    d) Data normalization
2. Which challenge is frequently faced in accounting related to the interpretation of financial statements?
    a) Inadequate financial reporting standards
    b) Complex tax regulations
    c) Difficulty in assessing liquidity.
    d) Ambiguity in revenue recognition
3. In finance, what is a common challenge associated with investment decision-making?
    a) Lack of financial modeling skills
    b) Difficulty in understanding economic policies.
    c) Market uncertainty and risk
    d) Insufficient knowledge of financial markets
4. What challenge often occurs in statistics when conducting surveys or experiments?
    a) Data visualization
    b) Sampling bias
    c) Data normalization
    d) Descriptive statistics
5. What is a shared challenge in finance and accounting related to regulatory compliance?
    a) Lack of financial modeling skills
    b) Changing accounting standards.

c) Market volatility

d) Difficulty in assessing liquidity.

6. In statistics, what challenge is associated with interpreting statistical results?

    a) Data security

    b) Selection bias

    c) Financial modeling

    d) Economic forecasting

7. What challenge is common to all three disciplines concerning technology integration?

    a) Limited access to financial data

    b) Difficulty in implementing statistical software.

    c) Data privacy concerns

    d) Keeping pace with technological advancements.

8. What challenge is often faced in finance regarding managing investment portfolios?

    a) Lack of financial modeling skills

    b) Inadequate risk management

    c) Market volatility

    d) Limited access to financial data

9. In accounting, what challenge is associated with preparing financial statements in a global context?

    a) Exchange rate fluctuations

    b) Difficulty in assessing liquidity.

    c) Inadequate financial reporting standards

    d) Limited access to financial data

10. What challenge is shared by all three disciplines regarding professional ethics and integrity?

    a) Lack of financial modeling skills

    b) Data normalization

c) Regulatory compliance

d) Upholding ethical standards

7.10 Answers to the Quiz and Explanation of Correct Answers

1. Answer B

Data accuracy and reliability are foundational principles that are crucial in the disciplines of statistics, accounting, and finance. Here's how each of these fields emphasizes the importance of accurate and reliable data:

Statistics:

Validity of Analysis:

In statistics, the validity of any analysis or inference is highly dependent on the accuracy and reliability of the data. Incorrect or unreliable data can lead to erroneous conclusions and misinterpretations.

Data Cleaning and Validation:

Statisticians engage in rigorous data cleaning and validation processes. This involves identifying and addressing errors, outliers, and inconsistencies in the data to ensure that statistical analyses are based on high-quality information.

Sampling Techniques:

When working with samples, statisticians emphasize the importance of random and representative sampling to ensure that the data accurately reflects the studied population.

Accounting:

Financial Reporting:

Accounting is dedicated to producing accurate and reliable financial statements. Financial reports, including balance sheets, income statements, and cash flow statements, serve as critical documents for decision-making, and their accuracy is paramount.

Internal Controls:

Accounting systems incorporate internal controls to safeguard the accuracy of financial data. These controls help prevent errors, fraud, and misstatements, ensuring the reliability of the financial information presented.

Auditing:

External and internal audits are standard practices in accounting to verify the accuracy and reliability of financial statements. Independent auditors assess whether financial information is presented fairly and following accounting principles.

Finance:

Investment Decision-Making:

In finance, decision-makers rely on accurate and reliable financial data for investment analysis. The accuracy of financial statements, market data, and economic indicators is critical for assessing investment opportunities.

Financial Modeling:

Finance professionals use financial models to project future scenarios and assess the financial implications of various decisions.

2. Answer D

Ambiguity in revenue recognition is a common challenge in accounting and can pose difficulties in interpreting financial statements. Revenue recognition is a critical accounting principle, and accurate and consistent application is essential for providing a clear and transparent picture of a company's financial performance.

3. Answer C

Market uncertainty and risk are pervasive financial challenges, significantly impacting investment decision-making. Financial markets are inherently uncertain and subject to various risks, and investors must navigate these uncertainties to make informed decisions.

Given these challenges, investors often employ risk management strategies, diversification, and thorough due diligence to make informed decisions and build resilient portfolios. Additionally, staying well-informed about market conditions and maintaining a long-term perspective are critical elements in navigating market uncertainty and risk.

4. Answer B

Addressing and minimizing sampling bias is crucial for ensuring the validity and reliability of statistical findings. Rigorous sampling methods, thoughtful study design, and awareness of potential biases are essential to high-quality statistical research.

5. Answer B

Changing accounting standards poses a shared challenge in finance and accounting, particularly concerning regulatory compliance. Accounting standards, such as the International Financial Reporting Standards (IFRS) and the Generally Accepted Accounting Principles (GAAP), undergo revisions and updates over time. These changes impact how companies prepare and present their financial statements.

6. Answer B

Addressing selection bias is crucial for obtaining reliable and valid statistical results. Statisticians and researchers must carefully consider the sampling methods' potential sources of bias and implement strategies to minimize or account for these biases in their analyses.

7. Answer D

Keeping pace with technological advancements is a common challenge shared by the statistics, accounting, and finance disciplines, especially when integrating new technologies into their practices. Embracing new technologies requires a proactive approach to learning, adaptation, and integration into existing practices to ensure continued effectiveness and relevance in an evolving landscape.

8. Answer C

Market volatility is a significant financial challenge, especially concerning managing investment portfolios. Market volatility refers to the degree of variation of trading prices over time, which can profoundly impact investment performance. Successful navigation of volatile markets requires strategic planning, risk management, adaptability, and a disciplined approach to investment decision-making.

9. Answer A

Exchange rate fluctuations can pose a challenge in accounting, particularly when preparing financial statements for multinational or global companies. Accounting professionals must carefully navigate the complexities associated with currency translation, hedging strategies, and compliance with accounting standards to ensure accurate and transparent financial reporting.

10. Answer D

Upholding ethical standards is a shared challenge across statistics, accounting, and finance. Ethical considerations are fundamental to maintaining public trust, ensuring integrity in decision-making, and fostering the responsible and fair practice of these professions. Ethical behavior is essential for maintaining trust, ensuring the integrity of analyses and financial reporting, and contributing to the overall well-being of individuals and society. Professionals in these disciplines must actively address and navigate ethical challenges to fulfill their roles responsibly and ethically.

General Summary

Profit and nonprofit organizations operate in intricate environments where effective management is critical for success. Utilizing statistics, accounting, and finance enables these organizations to make informed decisions, enhance performance, and achieve their objectives. By harnessing these tools, organizations can navigate challenges, capitalize on opportunities, and contribute to their stakeholders' welfare, whether driven by profit or a noble cause.

The synergy of statistics, accounting, and finance is pivotal in effective organizational management. While distinct in their focus and methodologies, the three disciplines come together to form a powerful trifecta that empowers managers to make informed decisions, optimize resource allocation, and drive the success of both profit and nonprofit organizations.

Statistics, as the science of data analysis, enables managers to uncover patterns, trends, and correlations within vast datasets. This provides valuable insights for strategic planning, risk assessment, and forecasting. Statistics aids in evidence-based decision-making, allowing managers to navigate complexities and uncertainties confidently.

Accounting is the bedrock of financial information, ensuring accurate recording and reporting of financial transactions. It gives managers a clear picture of the organization's financial health, allowing them to evaluate performance, control costs, and fulfill legal and regulatory requirements.

Conversely, finance takes a broader approach by focusing on financial planning, investment decisions, and risk management. It equips managers with the tools to optimize resource allocation, raise capital, and allocate funds wisely to achieve short-term and long-term objectives.

The seamless integration of statistics, accounting, and finance enables managers to tackle challenges with a comprehensive and data-driven approach. From budgeting and financial reporting to investment analysis and risk assessment, this synergy empowers managers to make well-informed choices that align with the organization's mission and strategic vision.

Furthermore, this trio of disciplines is crucial for profit-oriented organizations seeking sustainable growth and profitability and for nonprofit entities striving to fulfill their social missions effectively. Nonprofits can utilize the power of statistics to evaluate program effectiveness, accounting to maintain financial transparency and accountability, and finance to ensure responsible stewardship of resources.

Addressing challenges, such as data integration, technological proficiency, and ethical considerations, is essential for leveraging the full potential of statistics, accounting, and finance in organization management. By fostering collaboration among departments, embracing technological advancements, and upholding ethical standards, managers can harness the true power of this synergy to drive success and achieve organizational excellence.

The seamless integration and effective utilization of statistics, accounting, and finance create a solid foundation for successful organizational management. As these disciplines evolve and adapt to the changing business landscape, managers who embrace this synergy will be better equipped to navigate challenges, capitalize on opportunities, and steer their organizations toward sustainable growth and impact in an ever-competitive world.

References

1. ABC Assembly Inc. (2023). *We Are Electronic*. Retrieved from https://abcassembly.com/
2. Adebiyi, O. O. (2023). Exploring the impact of predictive analytics on accounting and auditing expertise: A Regression analysis of LinkedIn survey data. Available at SSRN 4626506.
3. Agarwal, S. A., Chauhan, N. K. S., & Ravikumar, S. (2024). *Basic Concepts of Research Methodology & Statistics*. Academic Guru Publishing House.
4. Aziz, F. (2023). *Beyond the Ledger: Enhancing Global Sustainability through Data-Driven Accounting Frameworks*. Farooq Aziz.
5. Black, K. (2023). *Business statistics: for contemporary decision making*. John Wiley & Sons.
6. Blye, M. L. (2020). *Reducing the Frequency and Effects of Fraudulent Activities in Community Action Agencies* (Doctoral dissertation, Walden University).
7. Burk, S., & Miner, G. (2023). It's All Analytics, Part III: The Applications of AI, Analytics, and Data Science. CRC Press.
8. Callahan, C. M. (2023). Evaluation for decision-making: The practitioner's guide to program evaluation. In *Systems and models for developing programs for the gifted and talented* (pp. 119-142). Routledge.
9. Cao, S. S., Jiang, W., Lei, L., & Zhou, Q. (2024). Applied AI for finance and accounting: Alternative data and opportunities. *Pacific-Basin Finance Journal*, 102307.
10. Chagadama, J. (2022). *Small Construction Business Owners' Strategies to Reduce Voluntary Employee Turnover* (Doctoral dissertation, Walden University).
11. Dhingra, R. (2022). *The Political Economy of Forced Displacement: Local, National, and International Responses* (Doctoral dissertation, Harvard University).
12. Dicke, L. A., & Ott, J. S. (Eds.). (2023). *Understanding nonprofit organizations: Governance, leadership, and management*. Taylor & Francis.
13. Feng, X. (2024). A Study of Systemic Risk in the Banking Industry. *Highlights in Business, Economics and Management*, *24*, 2416-2422.

14.Financial Statement of 7-Eleven (2014). PSC Annual Report SEC Form Retrieved from http://www.7eleven.com.ph/investors_relation.php?title=Annual+Report

15.International Salvation Council. (2023). *Missions and goals.* Retrieved from https://intersalvation.org/

16.Green, S. B., & Salkind, N. J. (2017). *Using SPSS for Windows and Macintosh: Analyzing and understanding data* (8th ed.). Upper Saddle River, NJ: Pearson

17.Harrou, F., Sun, Y., Hering, A. S., & Madakyaru, M. (2020). *Statistical process monitoring using advanced data-driven and deep learning approaches theory and practical applications*. Elsevier.

18.Huang, Y. C., Han, L. X., & Xie, W. H. (2024, March). Application of Big Data Analysis in Identifying Problems in Financial Reporting of BYD Company. In Modern Economic Management Forum (Vol. 2, No. 1).

19.Hussein, M. Q. S., Saeed, N. A., & Ahmad, G. S. (2023). Financial ratios analysis and companies' liquidity evaluation. *Journal of Global Economics and Business, 4*(14), 60-75.

20.Joshi, P., & India, U. (2023). Role of Financial Reporting Standards in Enhancing Transparency and Accountability: An Empirical Study.

21.JUBI, R. (2024). *Business Analytics-Unleashing Data-Driven Decision Making*. NEHAS PUBLICATIONS.

22.Kaplan, D. (2023). *Bayesian statistics for the social sciences*. Guilford Publications

23.Kasim, C., & Lobo, A. C. (2023). *Stockholder's Equity*. Available at SSRN 4511159

24.Kimmel,P.D., Weygandt, J.J., & Kieso, D.E. (2013). Financial accounting: Tools for Business Decision making (7th ed.). Danvers, MA: John Wiley & Sons, Inc.

25.Kimmel, P. D., Weygandt, J. J., Kieso, D. E., Mitchell, J. E., Trenholm, B., Irvine, W., & Burnley, C. D. (2023). *Financial accounting: Tools for business decision making*. John Wiley & Sons.

26.Kolassa, S., Rostami-Tabar, B., & Siemsen, E. (2023). *Demand forecasting for executives and professionals.* CRC Press.

27.Koutoupis, A. G., & Malisiovas, T. (2023). The effects of the internal control system on the US banking sector's risk, profitability, and compliance: A quantitative approach. *International Journal of Finance & Economics, 28*(2), 1638-1652.

28.Kwok, S., Omran, M., & Yu, P. (Eds.). (2024). *Harnessing Technology for Knowledge Transfer in Accountancy, Auditing, and Finance*. IGI Global.

29.Luamba, D. (2019). Strategies small business owners use to remain sustainable (Doctoral dissertation, Walden University)

30.Luamba, D. S., Blye, M. L., Mwema, I. E. M., Williams, I. A., James, K., & Chagadama, J. (2021). The benefits of innovation for small businesses. *International Journal of Business and Management Research, 9*(4), 425-432.

31.Luamba, D. S., Chagadama, J., Blye, M. L., & James, K. C. The Impacts of Audit Transparency on Increasing Trust in Nonprofit Organizations.

32.Madura, J. (2015). *International financial management* (12th ed.). Stamford: CT: Cengage

33.Major Competitors of 7-Eleven Retrieved from http://www.hoovers.com/competition.7-ELEVEN-INC.

34.Malinowski, M. (2023). Solvency and Debt of Rural Communes vs. Their Residents' Standards of Living: A Polish Case Study. *Agriculture, 13*(12), 2222.

35.Nasim, K. T. (2024). Accounting Practices of NGO: A study on MAX Foundation.

36.Non-Financial Factors for Investing in 7-eleven. Retrieved from http://www.accountantnextdoor.investment

37.Oh, D. M., & Pyrczak, F. (2023). *Making sense of statistics: A conceptual overview*. Routledge.

38.Raval, V. (2020). *Corporate governance: a pragmatic guide for auditors, directors, investors, and accountants*. CRC Press.

39.Rivera, R. (2020). *Principles of managerial statistics and data science*. John Wiley & Sons.

40.Peng, S. (2024). Registration Level and Nonprofit Foundation Efficiency in China: The Moderating Role of Organizational Income.

41.Privitera, G. J. (2023). *Statistics for the behavioral sciences*. Sage publications.

42.Prasad, S. (2023). Basic Concepts in Research and Data Analysis. In *Elementary Statistical Methods* (pp. 1-36). Singapore: Springer Nature Singapore.

43.Purnaningtyas, K. C. (2023). Analysis of Liquidity, Solvency, and Profitability Ratio to Assess the Financial Performance of PT Hamparan Estate Management in 2018-2020. JOBS (Journal Of Business Studies), 9(1), 11-22.

44. Shubbar, H. H. (2023). BANKING RISKS IN THE CONTEXT OF THE FINANCIAL CRISIS 2008. *World Bulletin of Management and Law*, 19, 136-142.
45. Star Light Consulting LLC. (2024). *About Our Firm*. Retrieved from https://gobrightstar.com/
46. Țîrcovnicu, G. I., & Hațegan, C. D. (2023). Integration of Artificial Intelligence in the Risk Management Process: An Analysis of Opportunities and Challenges. *Journal of Financial Studies, 8*(15), 198-214.
47. TripAdvisor, LLC (2023). *Ashville Hotels*. Retrieved from http://www.tripadvisor.com/hotels-g60742-Ashville_North_Carolina-Hotels.html
48. Turner, P. (2022). *Complementarity in Organizations: Strategy, Leadership, Management, Talent and Engagement in the Fourth Industrial Revolution*. Springer Nature.
49. Zapata-Cardona, L., & Martínez-Castro, C. A. (2023). Statistical modeling in teacher education. *Mathematical Thinking and Learning*, *25*(1), 64-78.

www.ingramcontent.com/pod-product-compliance
Lightning Source LLC
LaVergne TN
LVHW022052200926
848481LV00003B/876

* 9 7 9 8 8 9 2 4 8 3 0 9 4 *